AF425758

When Turning 13 Triggers the Devil

Angelina's Story
Fighting Abuse & Winning

A Novel for Young Teen
Girls

Dr. Dennis Ondrejka

When Turning 13 Triggers the Devil

Angelina's Story—Fighting Abuse & Winning
A Novel for Young Teen Girls

by Dr. Dennis Ondrejka

Published by **Page and Pixel**

ISBN: 979-8-89175-194-1 (Softcover)
ISBN: 979-8-89175-195-8 (eBook)

Printed in the United States of America

WHEN TURNING 13 TRIGGERS THE DEVIL

Angelina's Story: Fighting Abuse and Winning

A novel for young teen girls

---

*Studies indicate that 1 in 4 girls face sexual abuse before turning 18, with most incidents happening between ages 8 and 13, increasing around puberty. The predators' focus on age thirteen is deliberate—it marks both a legal boundary in many cultural contexts and a psychological obsession with newly developing girls. The girls' sense of powerlessness is significant **(reporting often causes family upheaval, financial hardship, disbelief, and accusations against the girl),** but in this story, strength emerges from her growing solidarity with other girls. The story begins with survival and tough times. It then shifts to Angelina's need to fight back—and she does.*

By Dr. Dennis Ondrejka

https://infograph.venngage.com/pl/RcGkKWGmy4
All pictures created by Dennis Ondrejka/ai

TABLE Of CONTENTS

A STORY THAT NEEDS TO BE TOLD

This isn't the story of one specific girl, but everything in it is real.

Right now—today, in your town, in your school, maybe even in the life of someone you know—girls are facing exactly what Angelina faces in these pages. I wish this were just an adult problem, something you could wait to understand later. But the truth is simpler and harder: it's never been an adults-only issue. It has always affected the vulnerable, the innocent, and those still discovering who they are.

Take Care of yourself

If this book becomes too heavy, stop reading. There's no medal for pushing through pain. Put it down, breathe, and come back when you're ready.

More importantly: talk about what you're reading with friends your age, trusted adults, and a counselor. The girls in this story survive because they stick together—the "Sweet Seven." You need your own version of that circle. This book contains information that could help keep you safe, but your emotional safety matters just as much.

What Grooming Really Means

You've probably heard this word without fully understanding it. Here's the truth:

Grooming is when someone slowly convinces you to accept things you would never accept if you saw the whole picture at once.

If someone showed you a photograph of a dangerous place and said, "Let's go there," you'd refuse instantly. But what if they took a different approach? What if they started by making you feel uniquely special, then gradually pushed your boundaries—so slowly you barely noticed? What if they made you feel indebted to them, convincing you that you wanted this, that it was your idea all along? What if they quietly separated you from anyone who might sound an alarm?

By the time you recognize the danger, you're already standing in it. You might not even see it as danger anymore because they've reshaped how you think.

This pattern appears in predatory relationships, cults, radical groups, and any situation where someone discourages independent thought "for the good of the group."

Why This book Exists

Some adults asked me, "Should young girls even read this?" Then those same adults admitted, "But if we want to help young teens understand these dangers, this is exactly the book they need."

Here's the uncomfortable truth: this problem is ancient. For thousands of years, across cultures and eras, what we now recognize as abuse was accepted as normal. Some ancient religious texts even reflect these attitudes. We've inherited generations of acceptance of things we now know are profoundly wrong.

That's heavy. But ignoring it doesn't protect you—it leaves you vulnerable. You deserve the truth.

Why Angelina's Story Matters

Angelina represents every girl navigating the bewildering space between twelve and fifteen, caught between childhood and adulthood.

"When Turning 13 Triggers the Devil" isn't just dramatic language—it's reality. Something shifts at this age. Predators know it. Parents fear it. Girls feel it but don't always understand it.

Thirteen isn't magical, but it's often when your body changes in ways that attract unwanted attention; when you crave independence yet still need protection; when you're discovering your identity and can be influenced more easily than you realize; when predators begin to see you differently; and when the confusion between being genuinely valued and being strategically used becomes most dangerous.

We Can Change This Story

I need your help to support all the Angelinas out there. With the right people—with groups like the Sweet Seven, with aware adults, with girls who understand these dangers and protect each other—we can interrupt this ancient pattern.

You're not powerless. Understanding what grooming looks like is your first line of defense. Read with awareness. Talk with people you trust. Watch out for each other.

You're not alone.

(Note: Yes, boys face their own dangers and need their own stories. Their vulnerabilities differ, and predators use different tactics against them. That story is coming. This book focuses on girls because the grooming patterns used against young girls have been refined over millennia. We need to illuminate those specific tactics.)

Respectfully,

Dr. Dennis

ACKNOWLEDGEMENT & DEDICATION

To Every Girl Reading This

This book came to me during a quiet meditation, when something deep inside whispered that I needed to write about something uncomfortable, something real, something that's been happening for over 2,000 years and is still happening today.

You've probably heard about Jeffrey Epstein in the news. What he did—what I call "the Epstein Devil's Matrix"—hurt over a thousand young girls. But here's what makes it even worse: for years, adults who should have protected these girls looked the other way. They buried the stories. They pretended not to see. They failed in their most basic duty to keep young people safe.

This wasn't just one bad person. It was a system—a trap designed to use young girls as bait to control powerful people's lives.

I wish I didn't have to write this book. I cried while writing it. My soul aches knowing these stories are real, not fiction.

Why This Matters to you

Here's the hard truth: in ancient times, hurting innocent young people wasn't used for blackmail because powerful people didn't think it was wrong. That might seem impossible to believe, but think about what people have "normalized" even in our own time—things we look back on now and say, "How did we ever think that was okay?"

Things change slowly. But they do change. And you're part of that change.

To the Survivors

To every girl who has walked this painful path, who has lived through what Angelina experiences in these pages: I send you my deepest love, my blessings, and my prayers. You are braver than you know. Stronger than they told you. More valuable than they treated you.

You deserved better. You still deserve better. And you're not alone.

Special Thanks

Several brave readers helped shape this book by sharing just how challenging it would be for young girls to read Angelina's story. They helped me understand what you need to hear—and what you need to feel understood.

Special thanks to my official readers:

- **Lara Mendoza** – for keeping me focused and steady when this story felt too heavy to carry alone
- **Tawnya Schar** – for your honest feedback and support
- **Terri Ondrejka** – for helping me see this through young eyes

I can't imagine exactly how this book will land with you, dear reader. But I know it's necessary. Because silence protects predators. And your voice—your awareness—your strength? That protects you and the girls around you.

This book Is Dedicated To:

Every Angelina around the world who didn't make it through this battle. You mattered. Your story matters. You are not forgotten.

Every girl reading this right now who knows she needs to stay strong. You can do this. You're already doing it.

The Sweet Sevens everywhere—those groups of girls who look out for each other, who refuse to let anyone face this alone. May your seven grow into seventy, into seven hundred, into thousands of groups around the world, each one winning this fight against those who would harm you.

You are not alone.

You are not powerless.

You are the ones who will **bring this fiction to life**—for you and those around you.

CHAPTER ONE

CUBA TO LIBERTY CITY TO FISHER ISLAND

4.2 Miles, One Lifetime

The first thing Angelina ever learned about the world was that some people ride ferries to work, while others own the ferries. But for now, she is a baby, but her mother is trying to make it all work.

Her mother, Joslin, was now in Miami and heading to the plush homes on Fisher's Island. She was the woman who stood at the rail with a sleeping infant strapped to her chest, watching Miami's glittering skyline fade behind her as the private ferry cut through Biscayne Bay's greenish-blue water toward Fisher Island—that sliver of manicured paradise where the average resident was worth thirty million dollars and the average housekeeper was worth whatever her hands could earn. But that knowledge would come later. First came the beginning, and every beginning is written in blood.

Angelina had just arrived in Liberty City, Florida, on July 17, 2011, at 3:47 a.m. Angelina Marquez-Santos entered the world in the charity ward of Jackson Memorial Hospital, sliding into the fluorescent-lit delivery room with a piercing cry that the overworked night nurse would later describe as "weirdly musical, like she was singing herself into existence." Joslin Marquez, twenty years old and thirty-seven hours into labor, heard only salvation in that sound.

She's here. She's alive. I didn't kill her by coming here.

The thoughts came in Spanish, always Spanish when Joslin was exhausted, scared, or remembering. The obstetrician—a tired resident who had delivered six babies that shift—placed the vernix-covered infant on Joslin's chest and said something in English that Joslin's panic-scrambled brain couldn't quite catch. Something about "healthy," "beautiful," and "congratulations."

"Congratulations."

A smile came from Joslin's employer, Marcella, who had only known Joslin for a few months, but said, "I am coming with you to the hospital. No one should do this alone." There was some type of small light, in all the darkness that came together for this moment. The nurse said, "Congratulations," and she finally heard the word, as if this baby girl were a prize Joslin had won, rather than the cost she had paid to survive.

SEVEN MONTHS AND SEVENTEEN DAYS EARLIER Somewhere in the Straits of Florida, December 5th, 2010. It was a time of desperation—and fear of being totally alone.

The smuggler's name was Esteban, and he smelled like diesel fuel, salt water, and the unique sweat of men who traffic in human desperation. His boat was a twenty-three-foot Mako center console that had once been white but now bore the gray patina of Caribbean sun and moral compromise. Seven people were crammed into a space meant for sport fishing: Joslin, three men from Pinar del Río, a mother with a five-year-old boy, and Esteban himself.

The mother paid in cash—American dollars saved for three years. The men from Pinar del Río paid with jewelry stolen from relatives.

Joslin had only a backpack containing three photographs—her parents before the hurricane, her parents after their wedding, and herself with a boy she had met three months earlier before leaving Cuba. She was only twenty years old and very happy living with her parents until the hurricane hit their home in Havana two months earlier. She worked at the hair salon where her mother also worked, and she knew she could do this type of work in Miami.

"You have nothing to pay with," Esteban had said in the darkness of the open water, trying to think of other ways for her to pay him. She did have a diamond ring that was her grandmother's, but she was not eager to give it up. "Nothing, Nenita?" She thought he might become angry with her, so she offered to get the money in Miami and then pay him. Esteban said he needed payment now. Something worth his time.

Joslin understood what he meant. She wasn't naive. She had heard the stories—everyone had heard the stories. The cost some women paid to get by. The price some men demanded just because they could, as the boat bounced along in the dark night, sometimes splashing water over the edge of the boat.

Behind her, across those ninety miles of dark water, lay Cuba and the collapsed house that had become her parents'; tomb and a boyfriend no one could find after Hurricane Paula tore through their neighborhood like God's own rage. The bodies had been buried six weeks earlier, except for her missing boyfriend, who could not be found. Joslin had stood in the rain at the funeral, water and tears indistinguishable on her face, and now—she understood with absolute clarity that there were two choices: die slowly in the rubble of her old life or risk dying quickly in pursuit of a new one.

"I can work," she'd said to Esteban. "When we get to Miami, I'll work. I'll pay you back."

He'd laughed, not unkindly. "Everyone says this. Then I never see them again. You disappear into Miami, and I am out three thousand dollars."

"Then what?" She'd forced herself to meet his eyes. "What do you want?"

She knew what he was thinking while standing there on that dock, where the smell of fish guts and motor oil mixed with the sweet rot of the tropical night. She knew it when she climbed into his boat. She knew it when he waited until they were an hour out, far enough that the lights of Cuba were gone and the lights of Florida were still a prayer away, and that is why she held onto the diamond ring—a last offering that may help her in this moment. "Tienes que venir conmigo."

Others on the boat became uncomfortable. The mother with the five-year-old looked away. The men from Pinar del Río suddenly found the horizon fascinating.

Joslin walked toward him and handed him the ring. Yes, it was valuable— at least close to the fee she needed. "That is what I have."

She turned away as he was going to argue the price, but she was already with the other passengers. Her face deliberately blank, her face tearing slightly but the alternative could have been worse—at least that's what she told herself as she rocked back and forth starting to feel very seasick.

She'd spent the rest of that crossing sitting as far from him as the small boat permitted, gazing at the phosphorescence in the boat's wake—those strange glowing organisms that appeared when the water was disturbed, transforming trauma into light. She watched those ghostly trails and thought her nausea seemed more than seasickness. I might be pregnant with a child from a man that no one could find. That's how these stories always go.

She'd been right.

She was at the Miami Hyatt Regency Skyline. It was a pleasant January morning in 2011 when she experienced morning sickness at exactly six weeks, right in the middle of her shift at the coffee shop near the hotel lobby.

Joslin landed the job three days after arriving in Miami, after sleeping rough in Bayfront Park and bathing in the public restrooms at Bayside Marketplace. The manager, an immigrant himself—Dominican, she thought, or maybe Puerto Rican—had taken one look at her desperate face and hired her despite her barely understandable English and complete lack of papers.

"Cash," he'd said simply. "You work hard, I pay cash. You don't work hard, you're gone. Comprendes?"

She'd comprehended perfectly.

For five weeks, she had been working opening shifts from 5 AM to 1 PM, learning to make lattes, cappuccinos, and those ridiculously complicated drinks Americans loved—half-caf venti soy no-foam extra-hot vanilla lattes with a pump of sugar-free hazelnut. She had learned to smile through exhaustion, anticipate what businessmen wanted before they asked, and discovered that the better her English became, the higher her tips.

She also realized that her period was late. Then she observed that her breasts felt tender. After that, certain smells—the hotel's signature coffee blend, the cleaning solution they used on the counters, men's cologne— made her stomach churn with visceral revolt.

The morning sickness hit her on a Tuesday, right after she steamed milk for a regular customer's cappuccino. The smell struck her like a fist, and she barely made it to the employee bathroom before her meager breakfast—a piece of toast made from day-old bread the hotel was throwing away— came back up.

When she came out, pale and trembling, the manager was waiting.

"You're pregnant," he'd said. Not a question.

She'd nodded, unable to lie.

"Can't have you puking around the customers." He sighed, not meanly, just practically. "I'll give you two more weeks, then you need to find something else. I'm sorry, mija. That's just how it is."

She had understood. She also realized that two weeks wouldn't be enough time to find another job, especially since she was showing more each day, had no papers, no references, and nothing but a growing belly and the face of a man named Esteban that she saw every time she closed her eyes.

That night, Marco Sethalan changed her life.

He was a late arrival—11:47 PM—walking into the hotel lobby looking exhausted, as if he'd spent the whole day making or losing big amounts of money. Joslin was about to close the coffee shop and already cleaning the counter when he showed up.

"You're closed," he'd said, gazing at her with eyes that truly saw her, not just looked through her like most hotel guests did.

Almost, sir. But I can make you something.

Just coffee. Black. And—" He glanced at the pastry case. "You've got anything left that's not three days old?"

She'd smiled despite her exhaustion. "One sandwich. Ham and cheese. I made it this morning for myself but didn't have time to eat it."

I'll take it. Sit with me while I eat, if you're allowed. I could use some conversation that's not about money.

She hesitated—was this even permitted? The manager had already left. The night auditor didn't care what happened in the lobby as long as no one died there.

"Okay," she'd said. "But my English is not so good."

"Your English is fine. And my Spanish is passable. We'll manage."

They had managed. For forty-five minutes, Marco Sethalan—though she didn't know his name yet, his Fisher Island address, his net worth, or the fact that his wife was in Paris buying furniture for their daughter's bedroom—had spoken to her like she was human. He asked her questions. Where was she from? (Cuba, she'd said simply.) How long had she been in Miami? (Seven weeks.) Did she like it here? (She looked at him for a long moment before replying: "I'm alive here. That's enough.")

He'd noticed, of course, what no amount of loose clothing could hide anymore. "You're pregnant."

Not a question. Not an accusation. Just an observation.

"Yes."

"The father?"

"Not here." The truest thing she could say.

He studied her face, and she had the strange feeling that he was solving an equation, with variables clicking into place. When he spoke again, his tone was careful, like people speak when they're about to change someone's life and want to make sure it's welcomed.

"My wife and I live on Fisher Island. Do you know it?"

"No, sir."

It's a private island—very secure and exclusive. My wife, Marcela, has been looking for someone to help with the house. Someone trustworthy who can also assist with our kids—simple tasks like picking them up from school. The woman we had before moved back to Colombia to take care of her mother.

Joslin felt her heart start to pound, that terrible flutter of hope that hurts more than despair because hope can be snatched away.

"I don't have papers," she'd said quietly. "I can't—"

"I have contacts," he'd interrupted, not unkindly. "People who can help with that. It takes time, but it's possible. In the meantime, we can pay you in cash, provide a room. You'd be safe there, you and your baby. Marcela's a good woman. She'd take care of you."

She'd stared at him, looking for the catch, the price, the 'ven acá nenita' that always lurked beneath men's generosity. But his face had shown only a kind of tired kindness, an expression of someone who had seen enough of the world's brutality to recognize when a small mercy was possible.

"Why?" she'd whispered.

He'd smiled, sad and knowing. "Because my mother came here from Argentina with nothing. Because someone helped her when they didn't have to. Because I can, and it costs me almost nothing to do so." He'd paused. "And because you make the best Cuban coffee I've had outside of Havana, and I'm a practical man who appreciates quality service."

She'd laughed then, surprised by the absurdity and relief of it. "I don't know how to work in a big house."

You'll learn. My wife is particular about things, but she's not cruel. She'll teach you," he said as he pulled out a business card and wrote something on the back. "This is my number. Think about it tonight. Call me tomorrow if you want the job. If you don't, no hard feelings. But the offer's genuine.

She'd taken the card with shaking hands.

She'd called him at 6 AM the next morning.

Joslin had no idea what living on Fisher Island would be like. *Maybe I could stay there for a year to settle in—and papers? Wow. That would be nice.* The Sethalan house was a Mediterranean revival dream painted in shades of coral and cream, with a red barrel-tile roof and huge windows that made the entire house a kaleidoscope of light and water.

It sat on a well-kept lot that included a pool, a dock with a thirty-foot sailboat, and gardens tended by Marcela Sethalan. She was graceful in a way typical of women who have never faced hardship—tall, slender, dressed in clothes more expensive than Joslin earned in a year in Cuba. But she was, as Marco had assured, not cruel. She was precise, yes. She had clear expectations for how she wanted things done. However, she was also fair, and once she realized Joslin was pregnant and alone, a nurturing efficiency took over.

"You'll stay in the guest cottage," Marcela said during that first interview, walking Joslin through the grounds. "It's small, but private. You'll take your meals with us—I insist on that. The children need to see different kinds of people, understand that not everyone lives like we do. And when the baby comes, we'll figure it out. There's plenty of space."

The cottage was eight hundred square feet of luxury that Joslin struggled to understand: a bedroom, a bathroom with heated floors, and a small kitchen she didn't need because Marcela intended it for shared meals. The first night she slept there, Joslin cried into her pillow—partly from relief, partly from guilt that she felt so comfortable while her parents rested in Cuban graves, partly from the hormonal chaos of her second trimester, and then from the inability to leave during a hurricane. Mostly, her tears hit her pillow in awe, overwhelmed by the strange blessing of safety.

The children, Jewel and MJ, were curious about her at first but then quickly accepted her as part of the household, as children tend to do when adults show someone belongs. Jewel, ten years old with her mother's elegant features and her father's thoughtful eyes, began teaching Joslin English in the afternoons, proud to be the teacher for once. MJ, eight and restless, simply said that Joslin made better quesadillas than their last housekeeper and asked if she could make them every day, please.

Joslin had settled into a routine: morning cleaning, afternoon childcare, evening English lessons with Jewel and increasingly with Marcela, who was genuinely invested in Joslin's ability to succeed in America. Marco was often away on business, but when he was home, he was kind in his distracted way, asking about her health and making sure she had everything she needed.

True to his word, he had obtained a Social Security number and work authorization within three months. Joslin hadn't asked how and didn't want to know. Some gifts were better left unexamined.

Angelina was born in July, and Marcela drove her to the hospital herself, staying through the labor even though Joslin had insisted she didn't need to, that she could manage alone. But Marcela shook her head.

"No one should give birth alone," she'd said firmly. "I'll stay."

When they'd brought Joslin and the newborn Angelina back to Fisher Island, a bassinet was already set up in the cottage bedroom, along with clothes, bottles—everything. A gift basket sat on the counter with a card: Welcome to the world, Angelina. You're going to be loved. —The Sethalan Family

Joslin had cried again. It seemed like all she did in America was cry.

But these were different tears.

At age one—another July, but now in 2012—she was moving away from the small innocence of a baby. The thing about babies is they don't care about geography, economics, or immigration status. They care about milk, warmth, and the sound of their mother's heartbeat. Angelina cared about these things with the single-minded intensity of someone who'd been alive for exactly one year and found the world generally satisfactory.

She was a strange baby — not fussy, not difficult, just peculiar in ways Joslin couldn't quite explain. She didn't cry often, but when she did, her cries sounded musical, rising and falling in patterns that seemed almost deliberate. She was captivated by light—would watch sunlight dance through the pool water, tracing the patterns with eyes that looked far too focused for a baby.

The pediatrician said at her one-year checkup, "She's very observant." "Unusually so. Some babies are just wired to notice everything. It's a sign of intelligence, but it can also make them a bit intense. Don't be surprised if she's a handful when she gets older."

Joslin had nodded, watching Angelina observe the doctor's pen move across the prescription pad. Her daughter's eyes tracked each stroke, categorizing, memorizing.

What are you seeing? Joslin wondered. *What world are you building in that strange little mind?*

On Angelina's first birthday morning, Marcela hosted a small gathering—only the Sethalan family, Joslin, and her daughter. There was a cake with pink frosting and a single candle. Jewel and MJ sang loudly and off-key. Marco took photos. Marcela had bought presents—too many, including soft toys, board books, and little dresses.

When it came time to blow out the candle, Marcela held Angelina and helped her manage the puff of breath needed to extinguish the flame. The room went dark for just a second before the lights flickered back on, and in that brief darkness, Joslin saw her daughter's face illuminated by the dying flame.

Angelina wasn't looking at the cake.

She was watching the smoke curl upward, her face one of complete focus, as if she was memorizing the exact way it disappeared into the air.

There you are, Joslin thought. My strange, observant girl. What are you about to see that the rest of us overlook?

She didn't know it yet, but the answer would be: everything.

The things people pretend not to see. The patterns they refuse to acknowledge. The devils lurking in plain sight, waiting for girls to turn thirteen.

But that knowledge was still twelve years off.

For now, there was cake, laughter, and the unique glow of Fisher Island sunlight streaming through expensive windows. There was safety, for the moment.

There was a ferry that periodically carried them between worlds—from the cottage where they slept to the causeway leading back to Miami, and to the city where other stories unfolded for other people, stories of girls, men, and numbers that added up to tragedy, and groceries.

But not every day.

Not today.

Today, Angelina turned one, and the world was bright and full of patterns waiting to be discovered.

The Devil could wait.

He always did.

He knew how to count to thirteen.

END CHAPTER ONE

Author's Note: This chapter establishes Angelina's origin story while centering her mother's survival and agency. Joslin's difficult negotiation by the smuggler is named clearly but not graphically depicted, honoring the reality of what women endure while refusing to exploit trauma for narrative titillation. The Sethalan family represents the complicated nature of wealthy benevolence—genuine kindness that nevertheless exists within profoundly unequal power structures. Angelina's "strangeness" is being established early: her pattern recognition, her intense observation, her musicality. These traits will become both her vulnerability and her weapon as she approaches thirteen. The ferry becomes the central metaphor: the daily crossing between worlds, the vehicle that carries them toward both safety and exposure.

C H A P T E R   T W O

THE ROAD TRAVELED BY DEVILS

When Protection Becomes Lost

It seemed like a typical morning on Fisher Island on March 15, 2015, at 6:47 a.m. The thing about an apocalypse is that it always arrives during ordinary moments. Angelina was eating Cheerios—picking them up one at a time with her small fingers, arranging them in patterns on her highchair tray before eating them in a sequence only she understood. Three-year-olds are supposed to be chaotic, but Angelina had always been a creature of strange order, finding mathematics in breakfast cereal.

Joslin was making coffee, humming something her mother used to sing, when the sound started.

Not knocking. Battering.

The front door of the main house exploded inward with the particular violence of men who have legal permission to destroy things. Voices shouting in that aggressive official tone that turns "FBI, open up!" into a kind of sonic weapon.

Through the cottage window, Joslin watched it unfold like a movie she couldn't pause: agents swarming the property, Marco face-down on the driveway in his pajamas, Marcela screaming in Spanish and English both,

Jewel and MJ—now thirteen and eleven—being escorted out by a female agent whose expression tried for kind but landed on grimly procedural.

Angelina stopped arranging her Cheerios.

"Mama?" Her voice was small but steady. "Why are the police hurting Mr. Marco?"

Joslin had no answer. Wouldn't have one for some time.

What she possessed was a sinking certainty that safety was always temporary, that every blessing had an expiration date written in invisible ink, and that somewhere, somehow, she had known this was coming. You couldn't live the way the Sethalans lived—that much wealth, that much ease—without something being wrong somewhere in the chain of cause and effect.

She simply hadn't allowed herself to think about it.

An agent appeared at the cottage door. Young, Latino, with a professionally neutral face. "Ma'am, I need you to come with me. Bring the child. You're not under arrest, but we need to ask you some questions."

Questions?" Joslin's English had improved over the past four years, enough to detect the threat behind the courtesy. "I clean the house. I take care of the children. I don't know about—"

"Marco Sethalan's business activities. We know." He glanced at Angelina, who was staring at him with that unsettling focus she always had. "We know you're probably not involved. But we need to verify that. Standard procedure."

The standard procedure took six hours.

Six hours of questions in a room that reeked of industrial cleaning solution and fear. Six hours of Angelina sitting in a corner with a coloring book given by a sympathetic agent, her crayons moving in strange patterns—not coloring the pictures, but drawing her own geometries in the margins. Six hours of Joslin repeatedly explaining that she was the housekeeper, that Marco had helped her when she was pregnant and alone, that she'd never seen drugs, money, or anything else they thought she had seen.

By the time they released her—cleared her, apologized for the inconvenience, and handed her a card in case she "remembered anything"—the sun was setting, and Fisher Island was already taped off with crime scene barricades.

An agent gave her a ride back to the causeway instead of on the private ferry. The FBI had seized those as well.

"Your belongings from the cottage are in these bags," the agent said as he loaded three large duffel bags into the back of the government sedan. "Everything else is evidence. I'm sorry."

Joslin stayed silent. What was left to say?

She stood on the Miami side of the causeway with three-year-old Angelina, three duffel bags, and the $20,000 she had saved—money that had been in a bank account Marco helped her open, money the FBI had frozen and then released after confirming it was legitimately earned wages—and realized she was right back where she started.

But this time, she had a daughter.

As she thought with concern, *this time, I have more to lose.*

"Mama," Angelina said, her hand in Joslin's. "Where do we go now?"

Joslin looked down at her strange, serious child, at those eyes that always seemed to be calculating something just beyond the visible world.

"Home," she said, though she wasn't sure where that was anymore. "We go home."

Liberty City hadn't changed in four years, which only made it feel worse. Now it had been a month since she had to leave Fisher Island. The apartment Joslin found was in a complex called Palmview Gardens—a name that was almost mockingly aspirational, considering there were no palms and no real gardens—just cracked concrete and buildings the color of old bruises. Two bedrooms, $950 a month, a cost that would drain her savings faster than she liked to admit.

But it was just a roof. It had locks on the doors. The neighbors mainly kept to themselves. Most importantly, Leah lived next door. Leah Martinez was twenty-four, going on forty, with a kind of beauty that poverty and poor choices seemed to be actively trying to erase—fine bones beneath puffy skin, pretty eyes rimmed with the sleeplessness of someone who never quite felt safe. She introduced herself on the first day Joslin and Angelina moved in, appearing at the door with a shy smile and a plate of rice and beans.

Thought you might not have time to cook, with moving and all," she'd said. Her American-English was clear, but her cadence hinted that Spanish still influenced her thoughts. "I'm Leah. Next door."

"I'm Joslin. And this is Angelina."

Angelina had been standing half-hidden behind her mother's leg, studying Leah with that same intense focus she brought to everything. "You have purple on your arm," she'd announced.

Leah quickly pulled down her sleeve with a nervous laugh. "Oh, that. I have a blood disorder. Makes me bruise easily. Looks worse than it is."

Even at three, Angelina still seemed skeptical. But Joslin smiled gratefully, took the plate, and invited Leah in for coffee, and a friendship was born—like many urban friendships are—out of proximity, need, and the particular loneliness women face trying to survive in a city that doesn't care if they do.

Within a week, Joslin understood the essentials: Leah had been in Miami since she was seventeen, had no family she communicated with, and lived with her boyfriend, Dirk, who worked at a clinic doing x-rays and "took care of everything."

The way she expressed taking care of everything—carried a weight that Joslin understood. The weight of a woman whose gratitude for being looked after was indistinguishable from her fear of what might happen if she wasn't.

But Joslin was in no position to judge. She needed childcare, and Leah needed purpose. When Joslin suggested the arrangement—watching Angelina in exchange for some money, not a lot, but something—Leah had agreed with an eagerness that was almost painful.

"I'd love that," she'd said. "I love kids. And honestly, it gets lonely here during the day when Dirk's at work. It would be nice to have some company."

She'd glanced at a bruise on her wrist—yellow-green and fading—and Joslin had seen her doing the math: If I'm valuable, if I'm useful, maybe he'll be gentler.

Joslin understood math. Different situations, same equation.

"Then it's settled," she'd said. "I start at the hotel next week. We'll figure out a schedule."

Angelina had been observing both women with that eerie awareness she possessed, her three-year-old face unreadable.

"I like you," she finally said to Leah. "You smell like vanilla and sadness."

Leah laughed in surprise. "That's... weirdly accurate. I love vanilla candles."

And you are sad," Angelina had continued matter-of-factly. "The purple on your arms makes you sad."

The laughter had died. Leah had crouched down to Angelina's level, her smile now fragile. "You're a very smart little girl. Maybe too smart."

"I see patterns," Angelina had said, which was true but also impossible because three-year-olds didn't talk like that and didn't notice things that way.

Except Angelina did.

Joslin settled into as much comfort as she could find, returning to the Miami Hyatt Regency Skyline with her papers in hand and an open mind toward new job opportunities. She hoped this arrangement would continue to work with Leah. Her return to the hotel felt like going back in time— before Marco, before Fisher Island, before that brief period when life seemed secure. A Starbucks concession had replaced the coffee shop. However, the front desk still needed staff, and the manager remembered her. Within two weeks, she was working full-time in registration, her English now good enough to handle the computer system and the constant requests of business travelers and tourists.

The pay was better than at the coffee shop, but the hours were long. She worked from 7 AM to 3 PM most days, which meant dropping Angelina off at Leah's by 6:30, rushing home by 3:45, and trying to fit motherhood into the evening hours before exhaustion took over.

It worked. Just barely.

Angelina seemed to flourish under Leah's care. She was well-fed, clean, and happy. She talked about Ms. Leah teaching her colors and numbers, watching cartoons, and playing with the neighbor's cat that sometimes wandered into Leah's apartment.

Everything appeared to be okay.

Everything was fine until Dirk started coming home earlier. The first time Angelina met Dirk, she was three and a half years old and coloring at Leah's kitchen table when the door opened and a man walked in.

He was forty but looked both older and younger—the kind of aging that results from hard living rather than just time. His tanned skin suggested outdoor hobbies, his arms indicated he worked out, and his hair was thinning but still thick enough to style. He wore blue scrubs—the universal uniform of medical work—and carried himself with the confidence of men who've learned that confidence is ninety percent of getting what they want.

"Well, well," he said, looking at Angelina. "Who's this little princess?"

Leah quickly stood up, her body language immediately changing—smaller, more cautious. "This is Angelina. Joslin's daughter, from next door. I'm watching her while Joslin works."

"You didn't mention we were babysitting now." His tone wasn't quite angry, but it wasn't not angry either.

It's just during the day. She's very good—quiet. You won't even know she's here.

Dirk walked over to the table and crouched down to Angelina's level. His smile was wide and practiced. "Hi there, Angelina. I'm Dirk. I live here with Ms. Leah. Are you having fun?"

Angelina studied him the way she studied everything—with that unblinking focus that made adults uncomfortable. "You smell like hospital," she said finally.

He'd laughed, surprised. "That's because I work at a hospital. I take pictures of people's bones. X-rays. Do you know what those are?"

"Pictures of people's insides."

"Smart girl." He stood up and ruffled her hair. "Leah, she can stay. Long as she's not trouble. And actually—" He glanced at Leah, and something passed between them, some silent negotiation. "—might be nice to have a kid around. Keeps the place lively."

Leah's relief was clearly visible. "Thank you, baby. I knew you'd understand."

That night, when Joslin picked up Angelina, Leah was cheerful in a way Joslin hadn't seen before. "Dirk met Angelina. He thinks she's wonderful. Said she can come anytime."

Joslin felt relief wash over her. "That's good. That's really good. I was worried—"

"No need to worry," Leah had interrupted. "We're all set. Dirk even said he'd help out if I needed it. Like if I had to run to the store or something, he'd keep an eye on her."

Warning bells should have gone off.

They didn't.

Or if they did, Joslin was too exhausted, too grateful, too desperate to listen.

There is a concept that begins small and seems so innocent, but it often turns into a pattern for some men to develop behaviors we call "grooming." It starts small. It always starts small. A piece of candy Dirk brought home "just for Angelina." A stuffed animal he saw at the drugstore. A special cup with princesses on it. Little gifts that made a child feel seen, special, chosen.

"This is just for you," he'd say, crouching down to her level. "Because you're such a good girl. Not all kids get presents, you know. Only the special ones."

Angelina, at four years old, loved feeling unique. She was clever enough to realize she was different from other kids—spoke differently, thought differently, saw things they didn't see. But being different usually meant lonely. Dirk made 'different' mean special.

By age five, Dirk was often home when Angelina was there. His shifts at the clinic had changed, he said. More flexibility. He'd sit with her at the table while she colored, pointing out which crayons to use and praising her strange geometric patterns.

"You're an artist," he'd tell her. "A real artist. Your mama probably doesn't appreciate it like I do."

Leah seemed happier during those days. The bruises became less frequent. She smiled more often. Whatever calculation she had made about Angelina's presence improving her situation appeared to be correct.

"Dirk really loves having you around," she'd tell Angelina. "You're like the daughter he never had."

Age five was when the touching changed.

Nothing major. Just small boundary crossings. Sitting her on his lap while they watched TV. Running his fingers through her hair. Giving her shoulder rubs. Helping her with her shoes, his hands resting on legs.

"Does that feel good?" he'd ask. "I'm just helping. That's what friends do."

The bathroom visits began around that time as well.

"Ms. Leah's busy," he'd say when Angelina needed to pee. "I'll take you. Come on."

He'd stand in the doorway while she used the toilet. "Just making sure you don't fall in," he'd joke. Sometimes he'd help her wipe, his hands gentle but invasive, crossing lines Angelina didn't have words for yet.

"This is our secret helper time," he'd say. "Secrets between friends. If you tell your mama, she might think Ms. Leah isn't doing a good job watching you, and then you couldn't come here anymore. You want to keep coming here, right? Keep getting your special treats?"

Angelina still wanted to keep coming. Despite the strange touching, and the bathroom incident that made her feel uncomfortable in a way she couldn't explain, she liked Ms. Leah. She liked the routine and felt like she had a bigger family than just her mama.

So she kept the secrets.

By age six, the gifts came with clear conditions.

"This Barbie is just for you," Dirk would say, producing a new toy. "But remember, special presents are secrets. If you tell your mama, the presents stop. And I'd have to tell her that Ms. Leah wasn't watching you properly, and then everything changes. You don't want things to change, do you?"

The word "secrets" grew heavier, more valuable, and more risky.

Angelina gathered them like she gathered patterns—organizing them in her mind, trying to understand the rules. Some secrets felt exciting, like when Dirk let her have extra cookies. Some secrets felt wrong, such as when his hands moved in certain ways during the "shoulder rubs" or when he asked her to sit on his lap in ways that felt different from how her mama held her.

She learned to divide herself: the Angelina who received gifts and attention, and the Angelina who sensed that something was wrong but lacked the words for it.

The only person who might have noticed was Leah, and Leah was too grateful for the peace to look too closely.

Joslin had thrown a small party—just the two of them and Leah and Dirk, because who else was there? A cake from Publix with pink frosting. Six candles. Leah had made arroz con pollo. Dirk had brought a present wrapped in shiny paper—a tablet, which seemed extravagant, but he'd said he got it on sale, and Angelina was so smart, she deserved it.

"For educational games," he'd said, winking at Joslin. "Kids these days need to know technology."

Joslin politely said, "That's too much, Dirk. Really."

"Nonsense. She's special." He'd looked at Angelina with an expression that Joslin read as parental-like affection but was something else entirely. "Aren't you, princess?"

After they'd left, after the cake was eaten and the presents were opened, after Joslin had tucked Angelina into bed with a kiss and a whispered "Happy birthday, mi amor," Angelina lay in the darkness and sensed the change in the air.

Today was a very special birthday. It was Angelina's sixth birthday, September 17, 2017. But a truly special gift was waiting for her as she snuggled into bed, filled with cake and ice cream. The angels came that night and sat on her bed.

She'd always been sensitive to something—perhaps changes in atmosphere or pressure. Like how a room feels just before a thunderstorm. Her mama said she was like a mood barometer—always sensing when Joslin was sad even if she was pretending not to be, always knowing when something was wrong even if adults insisted everything was fine.

But this was unlike anything before.

The air in her room began to shimmer.

That's the only word six-year-old Angelina used for it: shimmer. Like heat waves off pavement, but without the heat. Like something was pushing through from somewhere else, pressing against the ordinary world until it gave way.

And then they were there.

Three figures made of light — not solid, but not transparent either. They looked like people, sort of. Like a candle flame that resembles a person if you squint. They glowed with colors Angelina didn't have names for, colors that seemed to exist in the spaces between the colors she knew.

She should have been afraid.

She wasn't

"Hello, Angelina," one of them said, and the voice came from inside her and outside her head simultaneously.

"Are you angels?" she whispered.

"We are what you need us to be," another replied. "Tonight, we are your birthday present. The real one."

"A gift?" Angelina asked.

"A journey. Would you like to go somewhere beautiful?"

Angelina reflected on the question. She thought about her small bedroom in the apartment that wasn't Fisher Island. She reflected on Dirk's hands and the secrets she carried. She thought about her mama working too hard and being too tired. She thought about how the world sometimes felt heavy, like gravity was too strong.

"Yes," she said. "I want to go somewhere beautiful."

The tallest figure reached out a hand made of light. "Then come. But understand: your body stays here. Only your spirit travels. And you can always return. This is important. No matter how far you go, you can always come back. Say it."

"I can always return."

"Good. Now take my hand."

Angelina reached out, and her small brown hand passed through the light-like form, then she was moving—not walking, not flying, but traveling in a way that didn't require a body. The ceiling of her bedroom dissolved. The apartment melted away. Liberty City vanished.

And suddenly she was in a field.

The most beautiful field she'd ever seen, surpassing Fisher Island's gardens and the pictures in Leah's apartment books. Flowers in every hue covered rolling hills that seemed to go on forever. The sky was golden, not from sunset, but from some other light that seemed to come from everywhere at once.

And children were playing.

Dozens of them, maybe hundreds, darting through the flowers, playing tag, laughing with a joy that seems almost gone from the world, if it ever existed. They ranged in age—some looked like toddlers, others like teenagers. But they all shared one quality: lightness. As if they'd set down burdens Angelina didn't even know children could carry.

"Can I play?" she asked the angels.

"Not yet," one said softly. "You're here to visit, not to stay. Your time to play will come, but not for many years. You have work to do first."

"What work?"

You'll know when it's time. But until then, you can visit. Whenever you need to, whenever the world feels too heavy, you can ask us to come. We'll take you to places like this. We'll remind you that beyond the hard things, beyond the scary things, beyond the confusing things, there is this. There is always this.

"Why me?" Angelina asked. "Why do I get to see this?"

The third angel, who had been silent until now, spoke: "Because you're going to need it. Because you see patterns others don't see, and some of those patterns will hurt to notice. Because there are devils in your story, Angelina, and you'll need to know there are also angels."

Angelina watched the children play. She desperately wanted to join them. But something inside her knew she couldn't. Not right now. She belonged back in her body, in her bedroom, in Liberty City, with all its weight, secrets, and complexities.

"I should go back," she said quietly.

"You can," the first angel confirmed. "Just ask. That's the only rule. Ask, and you return."

"I want to return now."

And she was back in her bed, her body exactly where she'd left it, although it now felt strange—heavier, more solid, like slipping into a coat after swimming. The angels were fading, their light growing dim.

"Will you come again?" she asked.

"Whenever you need us. Just call. We'll hear."

"How do I call?"

You already know. The same way you asked to come back. Just think it, and we'll come.

They disappeared, and Angelina was alone in her room with the streetlight filtering through the thin curtains and the sound of music thumping from someone's car outside and the reality of her six-year-old life with all its complications.

But something had changed.

She had experienced something real. Had traveled somewhere authentic, even if it wasn't a place you could drive to. Had received a gift that had nothing to do with tablets, Barbies, or candy.

She had evidence that there was more.

More than Liberty City. More than Dirk's uncomfortable touching. More than her mama's exhaustion. More than the secrets she carried.

There was another place she could go whenever she needed to.

It was the first time in her life that Angelina felt genuinely powerful.

She drifted off to sleep with a smile.

The year following Angelina's sixth birthday was a strange balance.

On one side of her life, Dirk's grooming intensified. The touching became more frequent and invasive. He trained her to keep secrets as if he'd done this many times before. He made her feel both special and uncomfortable. He gifted her things while crossing her boundaries. He was kind and predatory at the same time.

She learned to dissociate without knowing the term—letting her body stay in the room while her mind drifted elsewhere, to the field with the children or to the places the angels showed her.

On the other side: the angels came whenever she asked. At night, when the apartment was quiet. Sometimes during the day, when she was at Leah's and Dirk was at work and she could find a quiet corner. They took her to beautiful places—gardens, mountains, and oceans made of light. They showed her other children who glowed the way she was learning to glow. They told her she was stronger than she knew.

She learned to need both, in a way. Dirk's attention fulfilled a need for being seen, even if the seeing was flawed. The angels' attention fulfilled a need for transcendence, for proof that the flaw wasn't all there was.

Joslin noticed nothing. She was too busy surviving, too grateful that Leah and Dirk seemed so generous with their time, too exhausted to see what was happening in the spaces between her attention.

She did notice that Angelina sometimes appeared distant and dreamy. That she talked about "visiting friends" but couldn't explain where or who. That she drew pictures of places that didn't exist—fields full of flowers, children with light coming out of them, beings made of color.

"Such an imagination," Joslin would murmur, pinning another drawing to the refrigerator, not realizing she was looking at a map of her daughter's survival strategy.

Leah noticed the way Dirk sometimes looked at Angelina and told herself it was fatherly. She convinced herself he was just being affectionate. She reassured herself that as long as he was happy and the bruises remained gone, everything was okay.

She convinced herself so completely that she nearly believed it.

Dirk noticed that Angelina was becoming more compliant, learning the rules. In his mind, she was being "prepared" for what would come when she was older, when she turned thirteen, and when she became what he was waiting for her to become.

He was patient and capable of waiting.

Angelina stood at the school entrance, carrying a backpack almost as big as she was, her hand tightly clenched in her mother's. It was her first day at Liberty City Elementary, August 2018. She was about to start first grade, and she thought maybe this could be fun, even though fear nearly held her back. "You'll be fine, mi amor," Joslin said, crouching down. "You're so smart. You're the smartest six-year-old I know. The teacher is going to love you."

Angelina nodded, but she wasn't worried about the teacher. She had been reading since she was four—she taught herself using the tablet Dirk gave her, though she tried not to think about that. She could already do math that second-graders struggled with. School didn't scare her.

What scared her was leaving the routines she was familiar with. Even the bad ones. Even Dirk.

Because with Dirk, she understood the patterns. School was unfamiliar territory, with new variables and new people to meet.

"I know, Mama," she said. "I'll be good."

You're always good, Joslin said, kissing her forehead. "I'll pick you up at three. Ms. Leah will watch you for just three more months, okay? After that, you'll go to the after-school programs here."

"Three more months," she thought to herself, as she was filled with ideas about rethinking the time.

"Ninety days," but that number didn't feel any better.

Angelina's mind automatically calculated: about sixty-three days until Dirk would be home early. Sixty-three more chances for him to try to touch her. Sixty-three more times, she'd have to push his hands away and keep the secrets that were beginning to feel like stones in her stomach.

"Unless I make something change," she thought, and set the idea aside for later, for the angels, for the night.

"Go on," Joslin urged gently. "Your classroom is right there. Room 104. Mrs. Patterson. Remember?"

Angelina remembered everything—her gift and her curse.

She walked through the doors by herself.

Three months later, the afternoon ended and then started again like all the others at Leah and Dirk's house. Angelina sat at the kitchen table doing homework—reading comprehension worksheets that were far too easy, made for kids still sounding out words phonetically. She finished in ten minutes and was now drawing in the margins, creating geometric patterns that calmed something in her mind.

Dirk came home early. He now consistently arrived home early on Thursdays. Leah had started attending a support group on those afternoons—for what, Angelina wasn't sure. "Just grown-up stuff," Leah had said vaguely.

Which meant Angelina was alone with Dirk from 2:30 to 3:00 every Thursday.

Thirty minutes.

Thirty minutes passed, during which the touching grew more intense, and his hands found excuses to straighten her collar, adjust her hair, and "fix" her skirt.

"Hey there, princess," he said, his voice that special kind of cheerful that made Angelina's stomach tighten. "Working hard?"

"Just homework."

"Let me see." He came around behind her, looking over her shoulder, his hand settling on her back. Too low. Always too low.

Angelina froze suddenly, like prey animals do.

"This is good work," he said, his hand moving in small circles. "You're so smart. Such a special girl."

His other hand reached down, as if to point at something on her paper, but his fingers grazed her leg. Then her hip. Then—

She stood up suddenly, pushing the chair into him. "I need to use the bathroom."

"I can help—" Dirk called out.

"No." Her voice was sharp, older than six. "I don't need help anymore. I'm six. Six-year-olds don't need help in the bathroom."

Something flickered across his face. Irritation, quickly masked. "Of course. I was just being nice. You used to like it when I helped you."

"I didn't like it." The words came out clearly and definitively. "I never liked it. I just didn't know how to say no."

Dirk's expression changed—the mask slipping for just a moment, revealing something cold underneath. "That's not a nice thing to say. After everything I've done for you. All the presents, all the special things I do for you. I thought we were friends."

Friends shouldn't touch each other like that.

Like what? I was just—

"You know what you were doing." Angelina's voice was steady, her six-year-old body stiff with confidence that seemed borrowed from someone older. "You know it's wrong. That's why you make me keep secrets."

The silence lingered between them, tense and threatening.

Then Dirk's face softened into a sad smile as his tactics shifted. "I think you're confused, sweetheart. I would never do anything to hurt you. You know that, right? I care about you. But if you don't like me anymore, after all I've done for you, after all the gifts and the special treatment... well. That hurts my feelings. That hurts them a lot."

He was trying to make her feel guilty. Angelina recognized it. She'd seen him use it on Leah—"after all I do for you, this is how you treat me?" She remembered his words clearly.

But Angelina had spent the past year visiting angels and realizing that she was stronger than adults thought she was.

"I'm sorry your feelings are hurt," she said, even though she wasn't sorry at all. "But I don't want you to touch me anymore. Not my back. Not my legs. Not helping with the bathroom. Not fixing my skirt. None of it."

"You're being very ungrateful—"

I just want you to know I don't like that. She grabbed her backpack and said, "I'm going to wait outside for my mama. She'll be here in fifteen minutes."

She walked to the door, her heart pounding but her steps steady.

"Angelina." His voice stopped her. When she turned, his expression was unreadable. "You're not going to say anything to your mother about our... misunderstanding, are you? Because that would be very bad for Ms. Leah.

Your mama might not let you come here anymore, and Ms. Leah really needs the money."

There it was, the threat hidden in concern.

"I won't say anything," Angelina said. "But you don't touch me again. Ever."

She left before he could respond.

THAT NIGHT Angelina's bedroom 11:47 PM

Angelina lay in bed, staring at the ceiling, her mind racing with equations she didn't yet have words for. She'd stood up to Dirk, yes. But she didn't trust it to stop. Predators didn't just give up because a six-year-old said no. She'd learned enough to know that. A quick question popped into her mind that she couldn't answer: *"How did I know this? I think my angels are talking through my mouth. I need to talk to them."*

"I need help", she thought. "Real help." She laid on the bed with her palms facing the ceiling and closed her eyes, and then said in a quiet voice, "I need your help. Please come see me."

The air began to shimmer.

The angels arrived more quickly now than they had at first, as if the connection between her world and theirs had weakened with use. They appeared at the foot of her bed, three figures of light that made the drab apartment bedroom feel less ugly.

"You called," the tallest one said.

"I need help with Dirk," Angelina said without preamble. "He's still trying to touch me. I told him no today, but I don't think he'll stop. I don't think he wants to stop at all. I really told him what I didn't like, and I think one of you was helping me. Right?"

"We are always with you because you want us to be," another angel confirmed, and something in the angel's tone felt like it was full of superpowers. You are right about how some people do not want to stop hurting children, and this voice seemed sadder than anything six-year-olds should have to hear.

"Can you make him stop? Can you..." She hesitated, unsure how to ask for what she wanted. "Can you put a snake in his car? A big one. Like a python. To scare him?"

The angels' light flickered, almost like laughter. "We don't usually make snakes, little one. It might be better to have him hear a very bold voice that he will never forget. We can influence minds, thoughts, perceptions, and when he hears us, he will never forget our words."

Angelina processed this. "So you could make him think there's a snake?"

"We could. But we have something better. Tomorrow, when he goes to work, we'll make sure he hears voices. Not out loud—inside his head, where he can't ignore them. Voices that tell him he's being watched. That touching little girls is dangerous for him in many ways. That invisible eyes see everything he does."

"Will that work?" Angelina asked with that questioning mind that seemed like she was 20.

"For most people? No. Their rational mind would ignore it as stress or imagination. But Dirk?" The third angel's voice carried something like knowing the real Dirk. "Dirk already knows what he's doing is wrong. His conscience is buried, but not dead. Voices speaking to his buried guilt? Yes. That will work. He'll be terrified."

"You promise?" As she started to sink into the pillow, where sleep was waiting.

"We promise, but that does not mean he won't do this with someone else."

You're prioritizing yourself first. That's not selfishness—that's survival. And maybe, when you're older, when you're stronger, you'll find a way to stop men like him for good. But right now, you're six. Right now, survival is enough.

Angelina thought about this, about the girl who would come after her— whoever she might be, wherever she was. She thought about how many girls there must be, dealing with men like Dirk and keeping secrets that tasted like poison.

"I want to stop all of them someday," she said quietly. "All the Dirks. All the men who touch girls who can't say no."

"We know," the first angel said. "That's why we're here. That's why you can see us when most children can't. You're being prepared for something, Angelina. We don't know exactly what—your future is not fixed. You will be making many choices, and your path is still unclear. But you're meant for more than just survival."

"When I'm older?"

When you're older. For now, let us handle Dirk. Tomorrow, he'll hear the voices. By tomorrow night, he'll be too scared to come near you.

"Thank you." Angelina felt tears fill her eyes—relief, exhaustion, and the heavy burden of being six and having to think like this. "Can I... can I go to the field tonight? See the other children?" The pillow no longer made her sleepy as she remembered the beauty of the children's fields.

"Of course. That's why we're here."

They took her. Out of her body, out of Liberty City, out of the world where men touched girls and girls had to protect themselves to the field where children played without fear, where laughter wasn't complicated by adults who hurt children, where being six meant being six and nothing more.

She stayed until dawn.

When she woke up in her bed, her body stiff from sleeping motionless, she felt both rested and old—like a wise old woman emerging from the forest to bless all the children.

She was six years old, and she had negotiated with angels to stop a pedophile.

A normal childhood was not something she was ever going to have.

But she could manage what started as survival and is becoming something new.

Dirk was halfway to the clinic, driving the streets so familiar that the car almost drove itself when the voices began. At first, he thought it was the radio—some strange interference, voices bleeding through from another station. But when he checked, the radio was off.

The voices kept coming.

We see you, they whispered, layered and overlapping like a choir from hell. *We see what you do. We see what you want to do. We're watching you, Dirk. We're always watching.*

His hands clenched tightly on the steering wheel. *Stress. I must be feeling stressed*, he thought frantically. Angelina, who pushed back yesterday, had rattled him, making him anxious.

Touching little girls is dangerous, the voices kept warning. *Dangerous for you in many ways. The law. Prison. Men in prison who dislike men who touch children. We see you, Dirk. Invisible eyes are everywhere.*

He pulled over, heart pounding. Checked his phone—nothing. Looked around the car—empty. The voices were coming from inside his own head.

This is crazy, he thought. *I'm having a breakdown.*

You're having a reckoning, the voices replied, as if they could hear his thoughts. *You've been seen and recorded. Evidence exists. Touch that girl again, touch any girl again, and consequences will come. Do you understand?*

Dirk understood.

He realized that whether he was going crazy or something supernatural was happening, he was terrified. He realized that he suddenly felt exposed in a way he'd never felt before. He realized that if something could put voices in his head, what else could it do?

The voices faded after fifteen minutes, but the fear stayed.

By the time he arrived at work, he had made a decision: Angelina was too dangerous. Too articulate. Too willing to push back. And now, apparently, connected to something he didn't understand.

He would stay away.

Far away.

The relief he experienced from making this decision revealed everything he needed to understand about himself, but he didn't examine that truth too closely.

Men like Dirk never looked at themselves that closely.

When Joslin arrived to pick up Angelina, she found her daughter sitting on the concrete steps outside Leah and Dirk's apartment, backpack beside her for the second day in a row.

"Why are you out here again?"

"I wanted to wait for you," Angelina said simply.

"Did something happen?" Joslin's maternal radar pinged. "With Dirk?"

"No," Angelina said, and it was technically true. Nothing had happened today. "I just... I think I'm ready to go to the after-school program at school. I'm six now. I don't need a babysitter anymore."

Joslin studied her daughter's face, searching for something she couldn't quite name. "If something's wrong   "

"Nothing's wrong. I just want to be at school. With other kids."

It made sense. It was reasonable. Joslin nodded slowly. "Okay. We can start that next week. But you're sure Leah doesn't mind?"

"I'm sure, Mama."

The next day, Joslin told Leah the new arrangement. Leah looked simultaneously relieved and disappointed—the money had been helpful, but she'd noticed the tension between Dirk and Angelina. Better to end it now, before whatever was brewing came to a boil.

Dirk, when told, simply shrugged. "Kids grow up. She's probably embarrassed to need a babysitter. It's fine." The voice from yesterday's trip to work was still ringing in his head.

He never touched Angelina again. Never got close enough to try. When they passed in the hallway of the apartment complex, he'd nod from a distance and keep walking, his face carefully neutral.

Sometimes, late at night, he still heard whispers—reminders and warnings.

He found other outlets—different ways to satisfy his hunger. Mostly online, where the girls were pixels instead of flesh, and the consequences felt more distant.

He told himself that was better. Safer.

The angels disagreed, but they weren't there for him. They were there for Angelina.

One girl at a time.

One monster deterred at a time.

It wasn't justice, but it was an important step.

And each step was necessary.

Angelina noticed everything. The patterns were clearer now. She saw how Dirk looked at her, how Leah pretended not to see, and how her mama trusted too easily because she needed to. She understood how secrets built up like debts and how attention could be both a gift and a trap.

She saw, and she survived by splitting herself: the girl in the body that Dirk touched, and the girl who traveled to fields of light.

She learned to be two different people at once.

It was practice, though she didn't realize it yet, for the person she would need to become.

The individual capable of recognizing evil and calling it out.

The person who could survive being thirteen years old.

But that was still seven years away.

For now, she was seven years old, with invisible friends and visible devils, and she was learning how to navigate both.

She was learning the architecture of angels and demons.

She was learning to see the patterns no one else would name.

And somewhere deep in her strange, brilliant mind, a countdown had begun.

Eight.

Nine.

Ten

Eleven.

This is a strange time: eleven

The number of years when many body changes begin for many girls, but for others it would be one or two more years.

But Angelina wasn't aware of all these changes as yet. She was just turning eleven, and she could still visit the angels: for now, that was enough. For now.

END CHAPTER TWO

Author's Note: *This chapter navigates extremely difficult territory—the grooming of a child—while refusing to be gratuitous or exploitative. Dirk's predation is shown through realistic patterns that experts recognize: gift-giving, special attention, boundary violations that escalate gradually, isolation through secrets, and targeting a vulnerable child in a vulnerable family. Importantly, Angelina's "superpower" emerges not despite the abuse but alongside it—she develops her spiritual sensitivity and pattern recognition while being groomed, showing how children find ways to survive. The angels represent her dissociative capacity, her spiritual resilience, and her ability to access something beyond trauma. Whether they're "real" or a psychological survival mechanism is deliberately ambiguous—what matters is they give her power when she needs it most. The stage is now set for years 7-13, where the grooming will escalate and her awakening will deepen, preparing her for the confrontation that must come*

C H A P T E R   T H R E E

THE METAMORPHOSIS

Age 11 - Sixth Grade –Losing the Girl

The bathroom at Liberty City Middle School had become sacred ground. In this confessional, whispered truths passed between stalls and across sinks, where mirrors reflected not just faces but futures nobody had asked for.

Angelina stood in front of one such mirror, pulling her new training bra strap back onto her shoulder for the third time that morning. The thing was a traitor, constantly sliding, always announcing itself beneath her shirt like a neon sign flashing: *LOOK, SHE'S DIFFERENT NOW.*

"I hate this," she muttered.

"Hate what?" Maya emerged from a stall, her dark eyes knowing. Maya always knew. It was like she'd been given an instruction manual the rest of them were still waiting to receive.

"Everything. This." Angelina gestured vaguely at her chest, her body, the universe. "I just want to go back to summer. When we were still... us."

"We're still us." But Maya's voice carried the hollow ring of a lie they both recognized.

The door swung open and Sophie burst in, her blonde ponytail swinging, cheeks flushed from running. "Emergency Girls meeting. Now. Before the bell."

Within two minutes, they'd assembled: Maya, Sophie, and Angelina joined by Priya, whose dark hair fell in waves past her shoulders; Emma, quiet and observant with her sketchbook always nearby; Jasmine, who'd shot up three inches over the summer and now towered over them all; and Keisha, whose laugh could fill any room but who'd been laughing less lately.

Seven girls crowded into a space meant for bathroom breaks, not a major crisis.

"Okay," Sophie said, her voice dropping to that conspiratorial whisper they'd perfected. "We need to talk about what's happening to us."

"Everything's happening to us," Jasmine said, hunching her shoulders in that way she'd developed, trying to make herself smaller. "I'm literally a giant now. Boys keep asking if I play basketball."

"At least boys are talking to you," Emma said quietly. "They look at me like I'm still in elementary school."

"Trust me, you don't want them looking," Keisha cut in. "When they start looking, it feels... wrong. Like they're seeing something that doesn't belong to them."

Angelina felt that observation settle into her bones. Yes. Exactly that.

"My mom says it's just puberty," Priya offered, though her tone suggested she found this explanation insufficient. "She gave me a book. It had diagrams."

"Did it explain why it feels like we're losing ourselves?" Angelina asked.

Silence. The kind that holds weight.

Maya shifted against the sink, her scientist's mind visibly engaging. "It's hormones. Estrogen, primarily. Follicle-stimulating hormone. Luteinizing hormone. They're released by your pituitary gland—that's in your brain—and they trigger all these changes. Breast development, body hair, your period starting, all of it."

"But what triggers the triggers?" Sophie asked. "Like, why does it start when it starts?"

"There's a region of the brain called the hypothalamus," Maya continued, warming to her subject. "It's like a master clock. When you reach a certain age—and it's different for everyone—it starts releasing this hormone called GnRH, which basically tells your pituitary gland to wake up and start puberty. But nobody really knows exactly what tells the hypothalamus to start. Body weight might matter. Nutrition. Genetics. Maybe even stress."

"So our brains just decide one day to betray us," Jasmine said flatly.

"Kind of, yeah."

Two weeks later, the conversation picked up in fragments—during lunch, in hurried exchanges between classes, in texts that glowed in darkened bedrooms.

Sophie: *My mom took me shopping for real bras this weekend. I cried in the dressing room.*

Angelina: *Why?*

Sophie: *Because I looked at myself in the mirror and I didn't recognize who I saw. When did I stop being me?*

The question haunted Angelina through Thursday's math test, through Friday's soccer practice where her body felt foreign and awkward, through Saturday morning when she stood in her own bathroom, studying herself with clinical detachment.

She'd started doing this lately—looking. Trying to understand the geography of this new terrain.

By Monday, she had questions.

The bathroom summit reconvened. This time, Emma had brought her sketchbook, and she'd been drawing—anatomical studies, careful and precise.

"I've been researching," Emma said, flipping open to a page of diagrams that made Sophie's eyes widen. "Because Maya got me curious about how everything works. And I realized... I didn't actually know where everything was. Not really."

"Nobody tells you the details," Priya said. "My mom's book just had these weird cartoon drawings that didn't look like anything real."

Emma's drawings were different—accurate, labeled, somehow both scientific and respectful. "So there are three openings," she explained, pointing with her pencil. "The urethra is for peeing. It's tiny, really hard to see. Then there's the vaginal opening—that's where the period blood comes out, and it's also... well, for other things eventually. And then there's the anus. That's for, you know. Number two."

"Wait," Jasmine said slowly. "Three different places? I thought it was just two."

"Most people do," Emma said. "Nobody teaches us this. I had to look it up in my mom's nursing textbooks."

"So the pee hole and the period hole are different?" Keisha asked.

"Completely different. They're close together, but separate."

Angelina felt a strange mix of relief and indignation. Relief because finally, someone was explaining the actual mechanics. Indignation because why had no one told them this before? Why were they learning their own anatomy in a middle school bathroom?

"The vaginal opening is also where you'd use a tampon," Maya added. "When you're ready for that. If you're ready for that."

"I'm not ready for any of this," Sophie said, and several voices murmured agreement.

October brought the first period to their group.

Priya arrived at school pale and shaky, and they knew immediately. The knowledge passed between them like an electric current.

"It started this morning," she whispered at lunch. "My mom was all excited and weird about it. She called my grandmother. I wanted to die."

"Are you okay?" Angelina asked.

"I feel like I'm leaking. Like everyone can tell. Is it normal to feel this... aware of your body?"

"Everything about this is about being aware of your body," Maya said. "That's the worst part. Before, we just lived in our bodies. Now we have to think about them constantly. Is my pad showing? Does anyone smell anything? Am I walking weird? Do I look different?"

"Yes!" Jasmine nearly shouted it, then lowered her voice. "I'm always thinking about my body now. What it looks like. How much space it takes up. Whether I'm standing right or sitting right. It's exhausting."

By November, three more of them had started their periods. Only Angelina, Emma, and Jasmine remained in what Sophie had started calling "the before times."

The bathroom meetings had evolved. They compared notes now—about cramps (Keisha had them so bad she'd missed school), about flow (Maya's was light, Priya's heavy), about the logistics of changing pads during passing period (Sophie had perfected the art of the silent unwrap).

"Do you think we look different?" Emma asked one afternoon, her artist's eye studying each of them. "Like, really different? Or does it just feel that way?"

They lined up against the mirror, seven girls in descending height order, studying their reflections.

"We look older," Maya said finally. "Our faces are changing too. Losing that kid roundness."

"I miss my kid face," Sophie said softly.

"I miss not having to wear a bra," Jasmine added.

"I miss when boys didn't stare," Keisha said.

That observation shifted something in the air. They all felt it—the weight of male attention that had begun to settle on them like dust.

"Tyler and his friends have been rating girls," Priya said, her voice tight. "I heard them in the hallway. They give scores based on how developed you are."

"That's disgusting," Emma said.

"That's boys," Maya replied grimly.

By December, a hierarchy had indeed emerged, though none of them wanted to acknowledge it. The girls who'd developed more were treated differently—by boys, by other girls, sometimes even by teachers in ways so subtle they were hard to name.

Sophie, who'd been a late bloomer among them but was now decidedly not, had been asked out twice. She'd said no both times, but the fact of being asked had changed something. Created distance.

"It's not fair," Emma said one afternoon. Just the two of them, Angelina and Emma, still waiting for their bodies to betray them completely. "We're all the same people we've always been. Why does having bigger boobs make you more important?"

"Because boys are stupid," Angelina said.

"It's not just boys though. Some of the girls treat Sophie different now too. Like she's graduated to something we're not invited to yet."

Angelina had noticed. The Girls Club was still in need of a new name, but fault lines had appeared, subtle as earthquake warnings.

January brought Angelina's first period, arriving like a thief on a Tuesday morning during English class.

She felt it—the warmth, the wetness—and knew immediately. The bathroom confirmed her suspicion, a smear of red that felt both inevitable and shocking.

Her hands shook as she wrapped toilet paper around her underwear, a makeshift solution until she could get to the nurse's office. She felt tears burning behind her eyes but refused to let them fall.

This was it. The second-to-last domino to fall. Only Emma was left to surrender to the metamorphosis.

When she told the others at lunch, their faces held sympathy, solidarity, and something else: relief. Now they were all in it together again. The division between the befores and afters had closed.

"Welcome to the club nobody wanted to join," Maya said, squeezing her hand.

"Does it get better?" Angelina asked.

"You get used to it," Priya said. "That's not the same as better, but it's something."

February found them adapting, adjusting, and accommodating. They'd developed systems: extra supplies kept in each other's lockers, a shared stash of ibuprofen, code words for period emergencies. They'd become experts in their own bodies out of necessity, cartographers of uncharted territory.

But they'd also become guardians of something precious: each other's dignity in the face of change.

When Emma finally started her period in March, they surrounded her with the quiet competence of veterans. When Jasmine's breasts finally began to develop and she could no longer hide behind her height alone, they reminded her she was more than her body. When Sophie's early development attracted the wrong kind of attention from an eighth-grade boy, they stood between her and him like a wall.

Our group will need a new name, but for now, they were being forged in playgrounds and birthday parties, but they were being refined in something harder: the crucible of becoming.

One afternoon in late March, they gathered one last time in their bathroom sanctuary. Not for an emergency, but for a ritual they hadn't planned but all understood.

"We should promise something," Angelina said. "Before we get any older and forget what this felt like."

"Promise what?" Emma asked.

"That we'll remember," Keisha said slowly. "That this was hard. That our bodies changed but we're still us. That we didn't ask for any of this but we will survive this whenever it comes."

"Together," Maya added.

"That we'll never rate each other," Priya said fiercely. "That we'll never make another girl feel like her body is wrong or too much or not enough."

"That we'll tell our daughters the truth," Sophie said. "If we have daughters. About the three openings and the hormones and how none of it is shameful, even though everyone acts like it is."

"That we'll never forget what it felt like to be eleven," Jasmine added. "Standing on the edge of everything, terrified and hopeful and confused."

They joined hands in a circle, seven girls reflected seven times in the fluorescent-lit mirror. Still themselves. Already different. Forever changed. Now all at age twelve. We definitely need a new name.

"The Sweet Seven," Angelina said.

"The Sweet Seven," they echoed.

Outside, the bell rang, summoning them back to a world that wouldn't wait. But for one moment more, they stood together in the space between childhood and whatever came next, witnesses to each other's metamorphosis, guardians of each other's truth.

The bathroom door swung open, and they stepped through it—not into the past they'd lost, but into the future they'd face together.

Educational Note:

The bodily changes described in this chapter are a normal part of puberty, typically beginning between ages 8-13 for most girls, though the timing varies widely and all timelines are normal. These changes are triggered by hormonal shifts orchestrated by the hypothalamus and pituitary gland in the brain, which release hormones that signal the ovaries to begin producing estrogen and progesterone.

The physical changes include:

- *Breast development (thelarche)*
- *Growth spurts*
- *Development of body hair*
- *Onset of menstruation (menarche)*
- *Changes in body composition and fat distribution*
- *Skin changes, including acne*

Understanding female anatomy is crucial. The external female genitalia include three separate openings:

1. *The urethral opening (for urination)*
2. *The vaginal opening (for menstruation and, later, sexual activity and childbirth)*
3. *The anal opening (for defecation)*

Many young people are not taught these basic anatomical facts, leading to confusion and shame. Accurate, age-appropriate education about bodies and development helps young people understand and navigate puberty with confidence rather than fear.

If you're experiencing puberty and have questions, talk to a trusted adult, healthcare provider, or school counselor. What you're experiencing is normal, and you deserve accurate information and support.

CHAPTER FOUR

THE SWEET SEVEN

World's Worst Secrets

Angelina learned to hide her oddness by sixth grade. Six years had passed, and she had just celebrated another birthday that summer since most of the sixth graders turned 12. She was still at Liberty City Middle School when school started in September 2024. The classes were changing and some of the girls were going into different rooms and schedules for classes. They could no longer come together as one group. They decided to create different group support, but it needed to be with their homeroom groups.

The Sweet Seven, along with Angelina, Maya, and Keisha, started looking for others who needed a close-knit girls' support team. Emma, Sophie, Priva, and Jasmine, who were in the eighth-hour class, mentioned they could meet, when possible, but it was almost impossible during school due to scheduling conflicts. Angelina asked Priva if she could try to keep everyone together as much as possible, but they could do as they wished. We will need to do the same.

School was like that, not because it was necessary to split up friends, but because they were starting to have different levels and abilities. Eventually, they would be separated by a career-focused program in high school, but that was a couple of years away.

Angelina continued to see patterns everywhere—in math problems, in social dynamics, in the way teachers' eyes glazed over when they talked about standardized tests. She still visited the angels at night, though less frequently now. The field of children was always there when she needed it, but twelve-year-old problems felt too complicated to solve with spiritual traveling.

Twelve-year-old problems needed friends. This seems more typical — but it really wasn't that common. Angelina was never that typical.

She found four more friends simply because they would get together for lunch. After four weeks, Angelina, Maya, and Keisha introduced the other girls to the Sweet Seven. This name started as a joke when just learning about their bodies—seven girls, sweet twelve-year-olds, and the irony of claiming sweetness when they all felt raw and complicated. The name stuck because they needed something to call themselves. This identity felt chosen rather than given.

There was Maya—who was with the first group and kept her brilliant scientific mind, terrible at sitting still, always the first to laugh and the last to cry.

Rosa—quiet, artistic, the one who drew in her notebooks instead of taking notes, whose eyes saw things even Angelina sometimes missed, and had recently moved to Liberty City.

Keisha—loud, fearless, the kind of girl who'd fight you for looking at her friend wrong, who wore her toughness like armor over something more vulnerable. Sometimes she sounded like an angry trucker when cars cut right in front of them—words not expected in a twelve-year-old, and Angelina was already familiar with her rough edges from the previous group.

Jade—the one who'd started her period first, at age ten, and this was not something the previous group had encountered. She was similar to Priva who seemed older than the rest of them, who knew things about bodies and boys that felt like forbidden knowledge, except Priva avoided the boys like a disease. Jade seemed to enjoy all the attention.

Imani—gentle, spiritual in a Christian way that made Angelina's angel visits feel less weird, who talked about God like a friend she knew personally. This was new to any of the previous group, because Imani even prayed in the lunchroom before she ate her meals.

And Zara—new to the school this year, from somewhere else, somewhere that had hurt her in ways she didn't talk about, whose silence was louder than anyone else's words.

They found each other the way outsider girls always do—leaning on each other in the cafeteria, sharing a bond over being too smart or too weird or too much for the mainstream crowd. Within a month, they became inseparable. Within two months, they were confiding in each other with things they'd never told anyone.

It was Jade who'd suggested the Friday meetings.

"We should have something like a club— we are the Sweet Seven, after all."

"A club?" Maya had bounced in her seat. "What kind of club?"

"A real talk club," Jade had said seriously. "Where we can say anything. Ask anything. Without boys around, without adults judging. Just us." Jade was eager to have a place to talk about what was happening to her body and with boys—just too much change and no place to scream, cry, or say what she was feeling.

They'd all agreed immediately, with the intensity of twelve-year-old girls who'd been waiting their whole lives for exactly this kind of permission.

The Friday meetings began in November, when school ended at 2:00. By December, they'd become sacred.

Seven girls sprawled across Jade's bedroom floor—some on pillows, some on the worn carpet, with one (Keisha) upside down on the bed, legs against the wall because she said it helped blood flow to her brain, which helped her think. Who could argue with that?

They'd already covered the usual territory: school drama, annoying teachers, the boy in eighth grade who thought he was God's gift to all girls but was actually just annoying. Now they were in territory that felt more dangerous, more real.

Bodies.

"So like," Maya said, eating chips with the aggressive casualty of someone trying to sound casual, "are we all just gonna pretend we're not all going through weird stuff? With our bodies?"

Jade laughed. "What do you want to discuss? Periods? Boobs? The horror we feel in gym class when we're not sure how or what to wear—pretend boobs, real boobs, sports bra, no bra,"

"All of it," Angelina said quietly. She'd primarily been listening, as she often did, but this felt important. "We should talk about all of it. Because nobody else is telling us the truth." All the older women act like they were never 12.

"Amen," Imani said. "My mom just gave me a book. A *book*. Like that explains anything."

"My mom hasn't said anything at all," Rosa admitted. "I think she's hoping I won't notice my body changing if we don't talk about it."

Keisha snorted. "Good luck with that. These boobs are not exactly subtle." She gestured at her chest, which had indeed developed faster than the rest of the group's except for Jade.

"Have you—" Zara spoke for the first time in twenty minutes, her voice soft. "Have you all gotten your periods?"

Nods from Jade, Keisha. Maya, and Angelina. Head shaking "no" from everyone else, as words seem to be too real.

"I'm glad I'm not the only one," Zara continued. "Jade, when you said you got yours... did it feel like everything changed?"

Jade's expression sobered. "Yeah. It felt like... like I crossed some line. And suddenly, my uncle started making comments. About how I was 'becoming a woman.' About how I needed to 'be careful' around boys." She paused. "I was only eleven—but he said, 'wait til you are thirteen, then you'll understand how sexy you really are.' I wasn't even twelve yet, but he was weird about it. Like, I was hitting some magic number soon, and my mom had to tell everybody."

The room went quiet.

"My cousin said something similar," Keisha said slowly. "I'm turning thirteen in two weeks, and my older cousin said that is when girls become women. He's sixteen. It was... it was a weird conversation, and I thought to myself if he thought he was a man?"

Angelina felt something click in her mind. A pattern forming. "What exactly did he say?"

"He said that when I turn thirteen, I'll understand things differently. That I'll be ready to learn about relationships. Adult relationships."

Keisha's voice got smaller. "I told him I already knew about relationships from my parents, but he said that wasn't what he meant. And then my mom called us for dinner, and he stopped talking."

"That's creepy," Maya said flatly. "That's really creepy, Keisha."

I know. I know it is. But he's family. And he never really did anything. So what am I supposed to say?

Angelina's mind was racing now, patterns overlapping. Dirk and his grooming. Jade's uncle marking time by a girl's periods. Keisha's cousin is waiting for thirteen. The pieces were shaping into something she recognized but had never seen laid out so clearly.

"Can I ask something?" Angelina's voice was steady, but her heart was pounding. "Has anyone here... has anyone been touched down there?"

The silence was deafening.

Then, quietly, Rosa raised her hand along with Jade. Then Keisha. Then Zara, her eyes already filling with tears slowly raised her hand.

"Four out of seven. Wow!" Angelina calmly shook her head in sadness.

"Over half."

"Oh my god," Maya whispered. "Oh my *god*."

"I..." Zara started, then stopped. "I thought it was just me. I thought I was the only one who—" Her voice broke.

"Who what?" Angelina asked gently.

"Who let it happen? Who didn't stop it?" Zara was crying now, tears running down her face. "Since I was seven. Just touching at first. Fixing my clothes. Helping me with the bathroom when I was too old to need help. And I just... I let him. Because he was supposed to be nice to me. Because he gave me presents. Because I didn't know how to make it stop."

"That's grooming," Angelina said, and everyone looked at her. "That's what it's called. When adults do things gradually, make you feel special, then start touching, then make you keep secrets. It's called grooming. And it's not your fault."

"How do you know that?" Zara asked, her voice barely audible.

"Because it happened to me too." The words came out easier than Angelina expected. "When I was little. A man named Dirk. He babysat me. Did the same thing—presents, special attention, touching that escalated. I was six when I finally made it stop."

"How?" Zara's voice was desperate. "How did you make it stop?"

Angelina hesitated. She couldn't exactly explain the angels, the voices in Dirk's head. "I... I told him I knew what he was doing was wrong, and it needed to stop. It took more than that, but it is complicated to explain. I will tell you more as soon as I can figure out myself, and then I will tell the group."

"When I said that, it certainly wasn't enough," Zara said, and something in her tone made everyone turn to look at her. "It doesn't work when it's your father."

The room felt like all the air had been sucked out.

"Zara—" Imani started and stopped, "ah, ah".

"It's been happening since I was eight," Zara continued, staring at the floor. "That's why we moved here. My mom finally believed me. Finally left him. But it's already—" Her voice cracked. "I already started my period. And he told me that meant I was ready. Thirteen was when girls became women, and I was almost there, so it was time to 'teach me.' That's what he called it. Teaching."

Jade was openly sobbing now. Rosa had her arms wrapped around herself. Maya looked like she might throw up.

"My stepfather," Keisha said quietly. "Not all the way. Not... not sex. But close. And he keeps saying that when I turn thirteen, things will change. That I'll understand. That I'll want it." She looked up, her tough-girl mask completely gone, revealing the terrified twelve-year-old underneath. "He kept making me touch him, and when I said I didn't want to anymore, he said he would tell my mom I was already doing this for him. I don't want any of it. But I don't know how to make it stop. My mom says to be nice to him because he's nice to her, he pays the bills, and if I say something, he will blame me and everything will fall apart."

"Same," Rosa whispered. "My mom's boyfriend started last year. I tried to tell her. She said I was confused, that he's just affectionate, and that I'm imagining things because I'm jealous of her having a relationship."

"Jeepers," Maya said, and it wasn't her usual joking tone—this is terrible, a horror, a recognition that the world was worse than she'd thought. "This is... this is happening to all of you?"

"Not you?" Angelina asked.

No. I mean, weird comments from my dad's friend, but nothing... nothing like this." Maya looked around at her friends, and Angelina could see her recalculating the world in real-time. "I had no idea this was so common."

"Nobody talks about it," Angelina said. "That's why it keeps happening. We all keep secrets, thinking we're alone, but it's everywhere."

"What do we do?" Imani's voice trembled. "What are we supposed to do? Tell someone? But who? Who believes a twelve-year-old girl?"

And what happens after?" Keisha added. "Let's say someone believes us. Then what? Foster care? Homeless? My mom can't afford this place without him. Where do we go?"

The real horror of it weighed on them. It wasn't just about ending the abuse—it was about surviving what happened afterward. It was about balancing being touched with having a home, balancing violation with stability.

It was about being twelve years old and having to do math that would break an adult.

"I don't know," Angelina admitted. "I don't know what we do. But I know we can't just... we can't just let it keep happening. Not to us. Not to other girls."

"How do we stop it?" Jade asked. "We're twelve. We're kids. Nobody listens to kids."

Angelina reflected on the angels, the field of children, and the patterns she'd seen her entire life. She thought about how Dirk had stopped because he was afraid, but he probably just found other victims. She realized there are millions of Dirks, millions of girls like Zara, Keisha, Rosa, and Jade.

About how thirteen was approaching—for all of them—and how these men were sort of waiting, but had already spent years grooming.

"I don't know yet," she said slowly. "But maybe that's what this is for. This group. The Sweet Seven. Maybe we can figure it out together."

Figure out how to stop predators?" Maya's voice was skeptical. "We're in middle school."

"So?" Angelina met her eyes. "We're also the ones who know. We're the ones who see the pattern. We're the ones who have to live through it. Maybe that makes us exactly the right people to figure this out."

"You sound like a motivational poster," Keisha said, but there was hope in her voice, fragile and desperate.

I sound like someone who's tired of being prey," Angelina countered. "Aren't you?"

Nods all around.

Then we start by telling each other everything," Angelina continued. "No more secrets between us. Every weird comment, every touch, every threat—we document it. We tell each other. We look out for each other."

"And then what?" Rosa asked.

"I don't know yet. But we're twelve. We have almost a year before we all turn thirteen. Before they think we're—" She couldn't quite say it.

"Ready," Jade finished bitterly. "Before they think we're ready."

"So we have a year to get ready ourselves," Angelina said. "To plan. To prepare. To figure out how to fight back."

"Seven twelve-year-old girls against..." Imani trailed off, the enormity too big to name.

"Against the world," Angelina finished. "Yeah. I know. But we have each other. That's more than most girls have."

They sat in silence for a long moment, processing the enormity of what they'd just shared, what they'd just committed to.

Finally, Zara spoke. "The Sweet Seven," she said softly. "That's what we are. Seven girls who are going to figure this out."

"Seven girls who refuse to be victims," Keisha added.

"Seven girls who see the pattern," Angelina said.

"And who are going to break it," Maya finished.

They made a pact that night—documented in a journal that Jade kept hidden under her mattress. They wrote down their stories. They wrote down the names of the men. They wrote down the facts, the patterns, the ways these predators operated.

And they wrote down a promise: *We will **not let thirteen break us. We will kick the Devil's ass.***

None of them knew exactly what that meant yet.

But they had most of a year to figure it out, except Keisha, who was turning thirteen soon.

A few more months before the number that triggered the devil.

A few more months to become something other than prey.

The Sweet Seven had been born a month ago and now had grown up before it should have to.

The countdown had begun.

END CHAPTER fOUR

Author's Note: This chapter spans six crucial years, tracing Angelina's growth from a six-year-old learning to set boundaries to a twelve-year-old realizing her trauma is not unique but systemic. The Sweet Seven marks a crucial pivot—from isolated victims keeping secrets to a collective consciousness that sees and names the pattern. The statistics are horrifying but real: studies suggest 1 in 4 girls experience sexual abuse before age 18, with most abuse occurring between ages 8 and 12, escalating around the onset of puberty. The predators' focus on age thirteen is not coincidental—it represents both a legal threshold in many historical and cultural contexts and a psychological fixation on newly menstruating girls. The girls' powerlessness is real (reporting the abuse often leads to family disruption, financial crisis, disbelief, and further victimization), but so is their emerging solidarity—a sisterhood. We're now positioned for the final movement toward thirteen, where Angelina's supernatural gifts, analytical mind, and sisterhood of survivors will be tested against the devils who've been waiting.

C H A P T E R   F I V E

SURVIVAL BECOMES RESISTANCE

It was Friday, December 2024, at Jade's apartment. The **Sweet Seven** had now reached age thirteen, and the journal had become thick with documentation. Seven girls, seven stories, pages filled with dates, times, and descriptions written in careful handwriting that tried to stay clinical, trying not to let emotion bleed all over the evidence. But emotion seeped through anyway — in the pressure of pen strokes, in the words underlined three times, and in the occasional tear stain that made ink run like truth bleeding out.

They sat in their usual circle on Jade's bedroom floor, but the energy had shifted since their first meeting twelve months ago. They were all thirteen now—Zara was the last to turn, just three days ago—and crossing that milestone together made them both more vulnerable and more dangerous.

Thirteen. The number that hung over everything.

"So we're all officially women now," Maya said, her voice heavy with irony. "At least according to the assholes who've been waiting for this moment."

"Has it gotten worse?" Angelina asked quietly. "For everyone?"

Nods all around.

Jade spoke first, her voice calm and steady, as if she had told this story many times before, each telling making it a little easier to bear. "My uncle cornered me in the kitchen on my birthday. My actual birthday, not even waiting a day. He said that now that I was thirteen, now that I was a woman, things could 'progress' between us. That's the word he used. Progress. Like we were in some kind of relationship."

"My stepfather waited exactly one week after my period started," Keisha said. "Like he had a calendar marked. Showed up in my room at night. Said it was time for 'lessons.' I kicked him. Hard. He left, but..." Her jaw tightened. "He'll be back. They always come back."

Rosa had been crying quietly, and when she spoke, her voice was barely audible. "My mom's boyfriend gave me a gift. For turning thirteen—a necklace with a heart on it. Then he asked if I knew what it meant to give your heart to someone. Started talking about special relationships, about how some girls are mature enough at thirteen to understand adult love." She looked up, her eyes red. "I don't want his adult love. I don't want any of it."

"But we can't just say that and have it stop," Imani added. "I told my cousin I wasn't interested in learning about relationships from him. You know what he said? That I'd change my mind. That thirteen-year-old girls always think they know what they want until they try something new. Like my boundaries are just... just a phase he needs to wait out."

Zara had been silent, but when she finally spoke, everyone froze. Her mother and father had made up two months ago, and she allowed him to return and live in her house in Liberty City. He even left his job in Alabama to move here. I begged my mother not to let him, but she said he had changed and promised to behave only within what the Bible permits. His escalation had been the worst—and the most surprising, especially since he had been gone. Zara stated that he was now living in Liberty City, but she wasn't clear about how the arrangement was discussed with her mother—it did not include her voice at all.

"Within three days he said the time for preparation was over," she said, staring at her hands. "That thirteen was the biblical age. Mary was probably thirteen when she was pregnant with Jesus, because she was 14 when Jesus was born. Apparently, this was the Jewish custom of that time for all young girls. so if it was good enough for the mother of God, it was good enough for me." She screeched, a sound like an animal being hit by a car. "He used the Bible. The actual Bible. To justify raping his daughter."

"Did he—" Jade started.

"Almost. I locked my door. He broke the lock. I screamed. The neighbors called the police. He told them I was having a teenage breakdown, that I'd been acting out since my birthday, that I needed psychiatric help." Zara's voice was flat, with no emotion. "They believed him. They gave my mom the number for a teen crisis center and left."

"Jesus Christ," Maya whispered.

"That's when I knew," Zara continued. "The system isn't going to save us. Adults aren't going to save us. We're on our own."

Angelina had been listening with her mind working on multiple levels—the immediate horror of what her friends were experiencing, the larger pattern emerging, the historical weight pressing down on all of it.

"It's not just us," she said finally. "It's not just our abusers. There's something bigger happening. Something cultural, maybe even biological."

Everyone looked at her.

"Explain," Keisha said.

Angelina pulled out her phone, where she'd been compiling research for weeks. "I've been looking into the history. Across cultures, across time periods, thirteen is everywhere. At twelve, Jewish girls have their Bat Mitzvah—literally becoming responsible for their actions as adults. But it gets worse for the Ketubah culture when the girl is thirteen. She is now under a divine command from God to listen to her Father, who has set up a marriage for her. It's when Catholic girls are confirmed. In ancient Rome, girls could even marry at twelve. In medieval Europe, consummation of marriage was legal once a girl had her period, usually around thirteen or fourteen."

"Are you saying this is normal?" Rosa's voice was sharp with betrayal.

No. God, no. I'm saying there's a historical pattern predators are still following. Like they're running ancient software in their minds. Mary was probably thirteen or fourteen when she had Jesus—that's historically accurate. Girls were married off at thirteen in biblical times. In some cultures, first menstruation is celebrated because it means a girl can now be married and bear children.

She pulled up articles on her phone, scrolling quickly. "Look at this— quinceañera traditions, sweet sixteen, coming-of-age ceremonies across many cultures. They're all marking the same thing: the moment when a girl becomes sexually available. They dress it up as celebration, as maturity, as religious significance. But underneath? It's marking when men can access girls."

"That's sick," Imani said.

"It is. But it's also everywhere. And it's been everywhere for thousands of years. So when these men look at thirteen-year-old girls and suddenly escalate their predatory actions, they're not making it up out of nowhere. They're tapping into something ancient and horrible that society has been reinforcing forever."

"You think it's genetic?" Jade asked. "Like, programmed into some men?"

"I don't know if it's genetic or cultural or both. But I do know this—" Angelina looked around at her friends. "—we're not the first girls to face this. There have been billions of thirteen-year-old girls throughout history, and most of them had no choice. They were married off. They were raped. They were told it was normal, expected, godly even. We have more social support than they did, more options, but we're fighting against thousands of years of this being considered acceptable."

"So what do we do?" Maya asked. "If it's that big, that embedded, how the hell do seven thirteen-year-old girls fight that?"

"We start with what we can control," Angelina said. "Our own abusers. Our own safety. And then we expand from there."

She pulled out a printed plan—pages she'd been working on for weeks, refining each time another girl shared another horror story.

"We need a system. A network. A way to protect ourselves since no one else will."

They called it **Operation Red Alert**—red for danger, red for blood, red for the rage they all felt but had to channel into something useful.

The system was elegant in its simplicity:

Phase One: Documentation and Deterrence

Each girl kept their phone charged and accessible at all times. When a predator approached—entered a bedroom without permission, made an inappropriate comment, initiated any touching—the girl would send a code to the group chat. Just a single emoji: 🔴

The red circle meant: *Recording now. Initiate backup.*

The girl being victimized would quietly start her phone's voice recorder. Meanwhile, the other six girls would implement the staggered calling system:

- T+0 minutes: First girl calls 911, reports "Someone is attacking my friend at [address]," hangs up immediately.
- T+4 minutes: Second girl calls, same report, hangs up.
- T+8 minutes: Third girl calls, same report, hangs up.
- Pattern continues until police respond.

The theory was sound: multiple calls from different numbers reporting the same address would trigger a mandatory police response, even if each individual caller hung up quickly.

The practice was chaotic, terrifying, and surprisingly effective.

It was December 20, 2024 when the first test case was activated. Jade was in her room doing homework when her uncle entered without knocking—never knocked anymore, not since her birthday. He closed the door behind him with that deliberate softness that meant he was about to say something inappropriate, do something worse.

"Hey there, birthday girl," he said, even though her birthday was two weeks ago. "I've been thinking about our conversation. About you being a woman now."

Jade's hand was already moving toward her phone, concealed under her textbook. "I'm doing homework, Uncle Ray."

"This is more important than homework." He sat on her bed—with a familiarity that made her skin crawl. "This is about your education. Your real education."

The emoji went to six phones simultaneously.

"I don't want to talk about this." Jade's thumb hit the voice recorder. The phone was angled to catch audio, hidden but recording.

"You say that now, but you don't understand what you're missing. Thirteen-year-old girls think they know everything, but there's so much I could teach you—"

In six different locations across Liberty City, six girls were making phone calls.

"—and now that you're the right age, now that you're developed—"

"911, what's your emergency?"

"Someone is attacking my friend at 2847 Northwest 62nd Street, apartment 3B!" Maya's voice was panicked, perfectly pitched. She hung up.

"—we could have something special, something just between us—"

Uncle Ray was still talking, hadn't noticed Jade's attention split between his horrible words and the phone recording every syllable.

Four minutes later, another call. Keisha this time, same script, same panic, same hang-up.

"—your mother doesn't need to know. This is about you becoming a woman, and sometimes that requires—"

Four minutes after that, Rosa called.

By the time the police knocked on the apartment door—sixteen minutes after the first call, which was actually fast for Liberty City—Uncle Ray had left Jade's room, his face flushed and irritated that she wasn't being receptive, but he hadn't touched her yet. Not yet.

Jade heard her mother answer the door, confused. Heard the officers asking if everything was okay, if there had been a disturbance, they'd received multiple calls about an attack at this address.

"No, officer, everything's fine. My daughter's doing homework, my brother's here visiting. I don't know who would call about an attack."

"Can we speak to your daughter, ma'am?"

Jade emerged from her room, phone in her pocket, recording still running. "I'm fine. I don't know who called you."

The officers looked skeptical but found no evidence of wrongdoing. They took a report, reminded everyone to call if there were any problems, and left.

Uncle Ray was furious—not at the police, but at the disruption. He left shortly after, and Jade waited until she heard his car pull away before texting the group.

Jade immediately blurted out, "It worked. He didn't do anything because you called. The recording is clear."

"Did the police help?" Angelina asked.

Jade was joyful as she said, "No. But the calls disrupted him. He was in my room for 16 minutes. The recording is gold. He said everything. The age thing. The 'education' thing. All of it."

"So what now?" Maya was curious about whether they would continue to do the same each time.

"For now, we wait. If he tries again, we do it again. We explain to him why it's happening. He will quickly understand that having the police show up several times will be a problem. And if he goes too far, you will need to decide whether playing the tape with the police present will work, or whether we need another plan," Angelina continued.

Imani was angry and said, "I just feel we are too young to fight this crap. How can we…."

"I want to get an army of girls," Kesha began with a building frustration she hadn't felt before. "I wish we could walk with Pedophile Signs outside their houses when this happens. I'm so angry!"

Uncle Ray returned a week later, emboldened by Christmas and alcohol and the fact that Jade's mother was working a double shift at the hospital. He cornered Jade in the kitchen at 9 PM.

"We need to finish our conversation," he said, blocking the doorway.

"No, we don't."

"Don't be difficult. You're thirteen now. You're old enough to—you know."

Six phones began their staggered calls.

"—understand what men need, what I need"

Recording running.

"—and you're so pretty, so developed, it's not fair to tease me."

He reached for her, his hand going to her waist.

Police knocked on the door twelve minutes later.

This time, when Uncle Ray answered—Jade having slipped past him to her room—he was confronted with officers who were notably less patient.

"This is the second call to this address in a week. What's going on here?"

"Nothing. A misunderstanding. Probably kids pranking—"

"We need to speak with the minor in the residence."

Jade appeared, phone in hand, showing it was recording, pulled from her pocket. "I'm fine."

"Has anyone touched you inappropriately?"

She looked directly at Uncle Ray and saw the panic flash across his face. "Not this time."

"This time?" The female officer's attention sharpened.

"This time, the police came before he could do anything. Last time you came, and he stopped as well."

Uncle Ray's face went white. "She's confused, officer. She's going through a phase, being dramatic—"

"Sir, I'm going to need you to step outside."

After Jade's twenty-minute questioning—gentle questions from the female officer, whose name tag read J. MORRISON and whose eyes suggested she'd heard this story before—the police left with another report filed and a system notation of repeated calls to this address. REPORT: Suspicious predator by the name of Ray Dorn. The 13-year-old girl is named Jade, and she looks determined to confront her uncle. No formal complaint at this time and no actual abuse indicated.

Uncle Ray left right after that, but before he did, Jade met his gaze and said clearly: "This will happen every time you come into my room without permission. Every time you touch me. Every time you say anything inappropriate. The police will come. Always. I also have you on tape, and that will go to the police next time. Do you understand?"

He got in his car and left immediately.

Over the next month, Uncle Ray stopped visiting. He stopped calling. When he had to see Jade at family gatherings, he stayed across the room, his expression carefully neutral, the predator deterred by the threat of exposure.

It wasn't justice. But it was safety.

Not every confrontation ended with deterrence.

Zara's father didn't care about police calls. He'd talked his way out of them before. When Zara tried the recording-and-calling system, and the police came for the third time in two weeks, he did what cornered predators do when scared:

He got violent.

The belt came out after the police left. Zara took the beating in her room while her mother sobbed in the hallway, unable or unwilling to intervene. Red welts covered her back, arms, and legs. Punishment for "making me look bad," for "telling lies," for "bringing shame to the family."

The recording captured it all. The sound of leather on skin. Her screams. His rage.

The Sweet Seven met in an emergency session the next day. Zara could barely sit, the welts making every movement agony. Her mother told her to tell anyone who asked that she had just fallen. Her mother had pretended things would settle back to normal.

"The system doesn't work for me," Zara said quietly. "He's too far gone. Too violent. And my mom won't leave him. She's too scared of being alone, of being poor, of all of it."

"Then you need to leave," Angelina said.

"Where? I'm thirteen. Where do I go?"

It was the question that stopped everything. Where does a thirteen-year-old girl go when home is the danger? Foster care was a nightmare by all accounts—shuffling between strangers, often ending up in situations as bad or worse than what they'd left. Shelters were full. Relatives weren't safe—that's where the predators often were.

"There has to be something," Jade said. "Someone. Some adult who would help."

"Who?" Zara's voice was bitter. "Who helps thirteen-year-old girls? Really helps, not just files reports that go nowhere?"

The silence was answer enough. They looked at each other, and Imani said, "Let's all go to the Emergency Room right now." Zara's voice quickly responded, "They will want to call my mom, and even with the tape, my life will be left to Social Services and Foster Care. Not a good choice. Sorry Imani. Good idea if the system were different."

Rosa called her mom, and she agreed to let Zara stay with them for a while until they can work things out. Rosa told her mother that Zara's family has COVID and she needs to stay away for a few weeks.

"OK, Zara, you're coming to my place for a while. I have clothes that will fit." Everyone is relieved for the time being.

While they dealt with Zara's immediate danger, Angelina had been diving deeper into the research, trying to understand the pattern they were caught in.

She was looking for the symptoms of a much larger problem, and just kept it to herself for now.

She presented her findings at their next Friday meeting, her phone connected to Jade's TV, showing a presentation she'd created.

"Jeffrey Epstein," she said, and the name alone made everyone tense. They'd all seen the news, the documentaries, the endless coverage of the dead predator and his powerful friends. "He preferred girls aged fourteen to sixteen. But his network started grooming them earlier. At thirteen. They all turned thirteen at some point."

Slide after slide of documentation: flight logs, victim testimonies, the island where the powerful went to rape children.

"And he's not unique. He is the only one we know about because he was caught. But look—" More slides. "International trafficking rings. "What is the most common age for girls who disappear?" she asked. " It is thirteen to fourteen What is the most common age for recruitment into prostitution? Wait, you don't have to guess, you know it is thirteen to fourteen. Thirteen to fourteen is also the most common age for sexual abuse online."

"Why?" Imani asked, though she didn't look like she wanted to know the answer.

"Because thirteen is when we're old enough to be sexually developed but young enough to be controlled. It's the optimal age for predators—we are developing adult bodies but child powerlessness. We're crossing the threshold from protected children to available women, and there's this window where we're vulnerable in a way younger kids aren't, and older teens aren't. Of course, they all are abused, but this age seems to be the big target."

"The Epstein thing wasn't just about one rich pedophile," Angelina continued. "It was about blackmail. Powerful men were filmed with underage girls, then those recordings were used to control them. There's evidence this pattern goes back decades—intelligence agencies using child sexual abuse as a control mechanism. Girls our age used as weapons to manipulate men into doing what the people with the recordings wanted."

"That's conspiracy theory territory," Maya said, but her voice lacked conviction.

"Is it?" Angelina pulled up more articles—mainstream news sources, not fringe websites. "Operation Midnight Climax—CIA program in the fifties, using sex workers and secretly filmed encounters for blackmail. The Franklin scandal in the eighties—allegations of children being used in a sex ring involving politicians. The Dutroux case in Belgium. The Westminster pedophile ring in the UK. Over and over, the same pattern: powerful men, young girls, filming, blackmail, coverups."

"And no one goes to jail," Keisha said flatly. "Because the people doing it are too connected, too protected."

"Right." Angelina continued. "Epstein is dead—maybe suicide, maybe murder. Who knows. Ghislaine Maxwell got twenty years, but that's just one person, and she's already been moved to minimal security. All those who raped and trafficked thousands of girls, and everyone who enabled it, are still free."

Rosa looked like she might cry. "So it's hopeless. Even when there's evidence and everyone knows, nothing happens to the powerful people doing it—what chance do we have? We're nobody. Our abusers aren't rich or connected, but they're still more powerful than we are."

"Maybe," Angelina said. "But we have what those girls didn't—we have each other. We have knowledge. We see the pattern. And we're fighting back before we disappear into it."

"By calling the police and scaring our abusers?" Jade's voice was skeptical. "That's not exactly fighting back. That's just... surviving. Barely."

"It's a start," Angelina insisted. "But you're right—it's not enough. We need more."

They met more often now, with Friday meetings complemented by lunch sessions at school, weekend strategy sessions, and constant group chat updates. The Sweet Seven Plus had become a resistance cell operating out of a middle school.

The new plan was more aggressive.

"We can't save ourselves by just reacting," Angelina explained, showing them pages of notes she'd compiled. "We need to be proactive. We need to make it harder for this to happen to other girls."

"How?" Zara asked. She had moved temporarily to Rosa's house—sleeping on the couch because her mother had finally agreed it was "safer" so she wouldn't get COVID. A positive for Rosa was that her mom's boyfriend was absent, with two girls always present.

"Three approaches," Angelina said. "First: Documentation for legal leverage. We keep recording, but we also find adults who will help us use the recordings appropriately."

"We tried that," Keisha said. "Most police don't care."

"Not police. Child advocates. Social workers. Female officers who specialize in this. And we don't ask them to arrest our abusers—we ask them to confront them with us. To witness the confrontation. To make clear that the abusers are being watched."

She pulled up a list—names and contact information she'd compiled from the county's child advocacy center, school resources, and online searches.

These women work with children who have been abused. They're not perfect—the system isn't perfect either. But some genuinely care. We approach each of them individually, explain what we're doing, and ask whether they'd be willing to join our intervention team. It might not succeed because they have a legal obligation to report the abuser and may not agree with our method.

"What's an intervention team?" Imani asked.

"Like addiction interventions," Angelina explained. "Where family confronts an addict with evidence and consequences. We do the same with our abusers. We bring an authority figure—a child advocate, a female cop, someone official—and we play the recordings. We say: This is what you've done. We have evidence. We're watching. If it happens again, the recording goes public. To your work. To your family. To everyone. If we can't get an adult to help us, then four of us will go together to confront the abuser, and we say that all of us have the recording."

"That's blackmail," Maya said.

"Yes," Angelina agreed calmly. "It is. We're using the same leverage they use on us—shame, exposure, fear of consequences. But we're doing it to stop abuse, not enable it."

"Will it work?"

"It worked on Jade's uncle. It might work on others.

"It won't work on everyone like my father. He is too far gone, too violent", as Zara presents a reminder of her story. "But for the others? It's worth trying."

The second approach was education.

"We write a book," Maya suggested. "About grooming. About the warning signs. About what to do. Not for adults—books for adults already exist and adults don't read them or don't care. We write it for girls. For eleven- to fifteen-year-olds who are approaching or just past thirteen. We tell them what's coming. We give them the language to name it. We give them strategies to protect themselves."

"Who publishes a book by thirteen-year-olds about child sexual abuse?" Rosa asked.

"We do," Angelina said. "Self-publishing. It's not hard anymore. We write it together, each of us contributing chapters. Maybe an older sister can edit the book—there are free editing services online as well. We publish it as an ebook and print copies. We distribute it to every middle-school in our area."

"Schools won't let us distribute a book about sexual abuse," Keisha said.

"Not officially. But we can leave copies in bathrooms, in the library, in places where girls find them. We can share it online. We can post on Social media what to look for and where the books are. We can make it go viral if we're smart about it."

"And say what?" Jade asked. "That a bunch of thirteen-year-olds wrote a book about how men are grooming them? We'll sound crazy."

"We'll sound like survivors," Angelina and Rosa corrected in unison."

The third approach was the support groups.

"We can't be the only girls this is happening to," Angelina said. "If four out of seven of us have been abused or are being abused, that's more than fifty percent. If that's representative, there are hundreds of girls in our school alone who are dealing with this."

"So we start more groups," Imani said, understanding. "Like ours, but open to more girls."

"Exactly. We put up flyers—vague enough to get past administration, specific enough that girls who need it will understand. Something like: 'Thirteen? Need support? Friday lunch, room TBD.' We get permission to use a classroom. We facilitate groups where girls can talk, share, learn the warning signs, document their experiences."

"That's ambitious," Maya said, but she was nodding. "That's really ambitious. And might actually help people."

"It has to," Angelina said simply. "Because the alternative is letting this keep happening. To us, to our friends, to every girl who turns thirteen and suddenly becomes prey."

They voted. Ten hands went up. Sweet Seven and three other who had joined their group this year and are learning more than they ever expected.

The plan was approved.

The next three months were a blur of activity that would have been impressive for adults, let alone thirteen-year-olds juggling schoolwork and family dysfunction and their own trauma.

The Intervention Team:

They approached twelve different women—child advocates, counselors, female police officers. Eight said no, citing liability issues or policy restrictions or simple discomfort with the plan.

Four said and supportive yes. They could not threaten anyone, and actually preferred to be outside, letting the perpetrator know there was someone who would have to call the police and take them to jail if they called them into the house.

Officer Julia Morrison was the first—the same officer who responded to Jade's house twice. She met them at a coffee shop, listened to their plan, and said: "This is unorthodox as hell. I could get in trouble for this. But

I'm in. If I actually hear the tape, I have to take them to jail, so the idea of you girls playing the tape as a team of four with the adult staying outside just in case seems the best idea."

Non-police adults have a legal responsibility to call the police, so either way, if the adult gets involved, the person will be taken to jail. That creates another bunch of problems the girls were trying to avoid.

She was joined by Lisa Chen, a social worker at the advocacy center with fifteen years of experience working with abused children who was tired of seeing the same patterns repeated. Then Reverend Patricia Williams, who runs the youth program at a local church and believes in confronting sin directly. Finally, Dr. Yolanda Martinez, a psychologist specializing in sexual trauma, who was willing to donate her time to what she called "prevention interventions."

Together, they formed the core of what the girls called "The Secondary Witness Team"—adults ready to confront predators if the girls couldn't handle it on their own.

The Interventions:

Over three months, they conducted six formal interventions.

Keisha's stepfather was first. In the living room of their apartment, with Keisha's mother present (they'd convinced her by playing a recording that left no ambiguity), Officer Morrison and Dr. Martinez stood outside the front door but could be seen through the screen door. John Daily looked like a cornered animal when Keisha played the audio of him propositioning her, touching her, telling her it was "their secret."

"You have two choices", Keisha said, her voice quivering and still bold. "Choice one: This recording goes to the district attorney or the police outside the door. We pursue charges. You go to trial, probably to prison, and your life is over. Choice two: You leave. You move out today. You stay away from me permanently. You get therapy—Dr. Martinez, who is also outside, will give you some referrals if you ask her. And then, we don't pursue charges. But if you come within fifty feet of this house again, if you contact me or hurt me in any way, the recording gets released. All the girls have copies."

He chose option two. Was gone by nightfall.

Keisha's mother cried for days, grieving the relationship and the financial support. But she didn't make Keisha leave. Didn't blame her. It was more than some mothers managed.

Similar interventions followed. Rosa's mother's boyfriend was already gone. Imani's cousin left the state. Jade's uncle got a second confrontation when he started texting Jade again, this time with Reverend Williams going in with the girls gave him a spiritual condemnation that left him shaking.

Two of the six men disappeared—moved away, cut contact, vanished from the girls' lives. Three accepted the therapy referral and, according to Dr. Martinez, actually showed up to sessions. One refused everything and threatened to sue, but when Officer Morrison explained what statutory rape charges would look like versus what they were offering, he backed down.

It wasn't perfect. None of them were guaranteed to stay away, to get better, to never hurt another girl. But six girls had breathing room they didn't have before.

It was something.

The book:

They wrote it collectively, meeting every Saturday for three months. Each girl contributed chapters:

- Angelina: "Understanding Grooming: The Pattern You Need to See"
- Jade: "When Family Members Are the Danger"
- Keisha: "Your Body, Your Boundaries: Saying No Even When It's Hard"
- Rosa: "When Adults Don't Believe You"

- Imani: "Faith and Abuse: When Religion Is Used Against You"
- Zara: "Emergency Strategies: Staying Safe in Unsafe Homes"
- Maya: "For Friends and Allies: How to Help Someone Being Groomed"

They called it *"Grooming Girls: A Survival Guide by Survivors."* The cover was simple—just the title in bold letters on a red background. Inside was 120 pages of hard-won knowledge, practical strategies, resource lists, and the kind of honesty that adults rarely gave to children about the dangers they faced.

They self-published it in April. Made it free as an ebook, available for download from a website they created. Printed fifty copies on the library's printer, paying for paper from money they'd pooled together.

The copies appeared in school bathrooms, the public library, the teen section of the bookstore, left strategically where girls would find them. The website got shared on social media—carefully, anonymously, through accounts that didn't link back to them directly.

Within a month, they'd gotten emails. Dozens of them. Girls from across Miami saying *I thought I was alone*, *This happened to me too*, *Thank you for naming it.*

The book wasn't going to stop all predators. But it was arming girls with knowledge. That had to count for something.

The Support Groups:

They called it "The Threshold Group," and the flyers were deliberately vague:

"Ages 12-14. Figuring out changes in your life and body. Need support from girls who understand. Fridays, lunch period, Library Room 237. All are welcome."

Twelve girls showed up the first week.

Twenty the second.

By the third week, the room was packed—thirty-seven girls, some crying, some angry, some just relieved to be in a space where they could talk about what was happening without being dismissed or blamed.

Not all of them were being abused. But all of them knew someone who was. All of them had experienced something—a comment, a touch, a look—that made them uncomfortable. All of them were navigating puberty in a world that sexualized their developing bodies while simultaneously telling them they were children who should be protected.

The twist of ideas was making them all a little crazy.

The Threshold Group became a space where the contradiction could be named, where girls could say I'm not ready for this attention and I shouldn't have to be without being told they were overreacting.

The Sweet Seven facilitated, with Dr. Martinez dropping in occasionally to provide adult oversight and professional guidance. They taught the other girls the warning signs of grooming. The documentation strategies. The intervention techniques.

They created a network.

By May, there were three Threshold Groups running at three different schools.

The movement was growing.

However, despite their efforts, some situations remained unsolvable. There seemed to be limits to human interventions. Zara's father continued to escalate. She couldn't go home. Her mother wouldn't press charges. The foster care system was backlogged by months. She was living between friends' couches, basically homeless at thirteen, her possessions in a backpack.

New girls showed up every week with new horror stories. Thirteen-year-olds being trafficked by older boyfriends. Twelve-year-olds being groomed online by men pretending to be teenagers. Fourteen-year-olds pregnant from abuse and being forced to carry to term because of the state's abortion restrictions.

The pattern was bigger than the five remaining girls could fight.

"We're drowning," Jade said at their Friday meeting in late May. "We save one girl, and ten more need help. We intervene with one predator, and we find out there are twenty more. It's like trying to empty the ocean with a bucket."

"So what do we do?" Rosa asked, exhausted. "Give up?"

"No," Angelina said, but her voice lacked its usual conviction. "We keep going. We help who we can. We document everything. We build the network. We—"

"We call in bigger guns," Zara interrupted, and everyone looked at her. "If human systems won't help us, we need something else."

"Like what?" Keisha asked. "The angels? Angelina's invisible friends?"

It was meant as a joke, but Zara wasn't laughing. Neither was Angelina.

"Actually," Angelina said slowly, "that's not the worst idea."

The room went silent.

"You're serious," Maya said. "You want to ask your imaginary friends to fight child predators."

"They're not imaginary," Angelina said, and her voice carried a certainty that made everyone pay attention. "They've helped me before. Helped stop Dirk when I was six. And they've told me, repeatedly, that I'm meant for something bigger. That there's work I'm supposed to do. Maybe this is it."

"That's crazy," Imani said, but she sounded uncertain. "Right? That's crazy. I believe in angels," Imani continued. "I believe in God. I pray every night. But I've never seen an angel. Never heard voices from heaven. Never been taken to fields of light."

"Maybe you weren't supposed to," Angelina said. "Maybe I was given this for a reason. And maybe that reason is exactly this moment, exactly this problem."

"So what?" Jade asked. "You ask your angels to smite all the pedophiles? Send lightning bolts? What's the plan?"

"I don't know," Angelina admitted. "I've never asked them for something this big. But I think... I think it's time to try."

They looked at each other, seven-plus, thirteen-year-old girls who'd seen too much, fought too hard, and were running out of human options.

"Okay," Zara said finally. "We've tried everything else. Why not ask for divine intervention? Can't hurt."

"When?" Keisha asked.

Angelina thought about it. "Tonight. All of us together. If the angels are real, if they're as powerful as they've shown me, then maybe they can do what we can't. Maybe they can actually stop this."

"And if they're not real?" Maya asked quietly. "If you've been hallucinating since you were six?"

"Then we're back where we started," Angelina said. "Still fighting with human tools. Still doing our best. Still saving who we can save." She paused, meeting each girl's eyes in turn. "But if they are real? Then tonight might change everything."

The Sweet Seven Plus agreed to meet at midnight. In the field behind the school, Ten girls who'd tried to fight the devil with documentation, intervention, and education.

Ten girls who were ready to try prayer.

Or magic.

Or whatever it was that happened when thirteen-year-old survivors asked invisible beings made of light to help them wage war against the darkness.

They didn't know if it would work. But they were out of other options. Sometimes, when human systems fail, you have to try the impossible. Sometimes, when you're thirteen and the devil has awakened, you have to call on angels.

Most would just hope they would answer. Angelina knew deep down they would answer, but what would they say?

END CHAPTER fIVE

Author's Note: This chapter shows both the power and limitations of human intervention. The girls' strategies are realistic—recording evidence, building support networks, finding sympathetic adults, creating educational resources—and these methods do help some victims. However, the systemic nature of the problem becomes clear: they're fighting against thousands of years of cultural acceptance, against institutional failures, and against predators who are often protected by family systems and complex legal structures.

The Epstein connection is historically accurate and important—it demonstrates how abuse of thirteen-year-old girls isn't just about individual predators but about organized exploitation at the highest levels. The girls' exhaustion is real; they're children fighting adult battles with insufficient resources. The turn toward supernatural intervention isn't abandoning reality—it's acknowledging that sometimes the problem is too big for human tools alone. Whether the angels can or will help remains to be seen, but the request itself is an act of true faith that feels earned after everything these girls have tried and sacrificed.

CHAPTER SIX

THE SKIES GET DARKER

The Sweet Seven Plus sat in their usual circle on Jade's bedroom floor, but the energy was different tonight. Heavier. More desperate.

They'd spent three months fighting—documenting, recording, calling police, conducting interventions. Some victories, yes. Jade's uncle had backed off. Keisha's stepfather had moved out. But for every girl they helped, three more appeared at their Threshold Groups with new horror stories.

And Zara... Zara was still sleeping on Jade's couch because going home meant facing her father. Rosa's mother still refused to believe her accusations about her boyfriend. Two new girls from their support group had disappeared because their mothers had moved away to try to escape using geography. One of the girls wanted to stay connected and start her own Threshold Group in another state. The second girl was nowhere to be found, and they heard that her mother had changed all the children's names with no past contacts allowed.

They knew that the ocean they were trying to drain with a bucket kept refilling faster than they could bail water. Still, they felt like they were doing something, and that felt good.

Jalin, a new girl who had just arrived at their school from Washington State, was sitting in the group for the fourth time.

As the girls checked in, they would say their first name and rate their vulnerability that day on a scale of **No, Some, yes, and Painful**. Jalin was already crying as she checked in, and Dr. Martinez said calmly, "That sounds like 'painful'."

Jalin said, "Yes, I have to say something. I cannot wait any longer," as it seemed she was waiting for the perfect support she would need. Dr.Martinez was present as usual every other Monday. This was a good time for Jalin to let things out. "Can I tell you what is happening to me?"

The question hung in the air of the small group room. Imani had her hand over her mouth. Angelina's eyes were empathetic invitations to speak.

Jalin wiped her face with the sleeve of my hoodie, but the tears kept coming. Three months of holding this inside, and now it was spilling out like water through a cracked dam.

"I am pregnant, and it is all my fault. I let him," Jalin whispered. "I thought he loved me, and I didn't know how to stop him."

Imani looked at her with intense shock, "I know it takes two people, and I believe you are thirteen. Is that right?

"Yes." Her eyes are less teary.

Dr. Martinez suggested she start from the beginning. "I think you have much more to say than "I'm pregnant. Go ahead, tell us."

Jalin story begins as they all listened with open hearts and some fear about what she was about to say.

> *I was living in Puyallup, WA. Nobody's heard of Puyallup*
> *unless you're from there. I listened to my neighbors say '*
> *It sits in the shadow of Mount Rainier, a small town where*
> *everyone knows your business and the local diner still*
> *serves coffee for a dollar fifty,' which I didn't really care*

about. What I hated was living outside of town, where the houses got smaller, and the yards got bigger. Nobody asked questions about the yelling coming from our house. They would just say, 'Oh, that's the Lawson place.'

My daddy used to work at Boeing. Good job. Union wages. He'd come home tired but happy, swing the twins — Malik and Mindi, just eight years old — up onto his shoulders and ask Mama what was for dinner. That was before the layoff. Before his daily drinking. Before everything changed.

The first time he hit my mom, I was eleven. I heard it from my bedroom — that sound you never forget, flesh against flesh, then my mom screamed, and then she was crying. I told myself it was an accident. Adults have arguments. It won't happen again.

But it did. Again and again, for two years. The drinking got worse after Boeing. Daddy said he was looking for work, but mostly he was looking at the bottom of a bottle. And when the bottle was empty, his hands found my mother's face.

I learned to read his moods like weather patterns. Learned which floorboards creaked. Learned to keep the twins quiet when his eyes went flat and mean.

The night everything shattered, I'd made the mistake of talking back. Something small — I don't even remember what. His belt came off so fast. I curled into a ball on the kitchen floor while leather bit into my back, my arms, anywhere I couldn't protect.

Mama tried to stop him. She always tried. And he grabbed the lamp from the side table — the one with the painted flowers she'd gotten from her grandmother — and swung it at her head.

She dropped like a puppet with cut strings.

Malik had just turned eight, but he called 911. He knew what to do. I was crawling toward the kitchen, trying to reach my mother, blood in my mouth from where I'd bitten my tongue.

The police, ambulance, and the world seem to be at my house. My Daddy was put in handcuffs. The twins were taken to Social Services for three days while Mama was in the hospital with a concussion, and I sat in a chair by her bed, my back burning with welts, wondering if this was finally the end of it.

It was. But not the way I hoped.

When Mama got out of the hospital, she made a decision. She was going to leave him. My mom's sister lived in Georgia — Aunt Patrice, who we'd only seen at funerals and the occasional Thanksgiving. She had a big house, a good job, and, most importantly, she was 2,000 miles away from my dad.

We left Puyallup on a Greyhound bus two weeks later, and my father was still in jail. Everything we owned fit in four suitcases and a cardboard box.

I thought we were running toward safety.

I didn't know I was running toward something worse.

My aunt lived in Riverbend, Georgia, and we arrived three days later.

The new high school was three times the size of my old one. I walked those halls like a ghost those first weeks — invisible, silent, flinching every time a locker slammed too loudly. Probably just like I was doing at this school

That's when Marcus found me.

He was seventeen. A senior. Captain of the basketball team with a smile that made the other girls whisper and giggle. I couldn't understand why someone like him would notice someone like me — a skinny eighth-grader with secondhand clothes and eyes that couldn't quite meet anyone else's. In that town, high school was grades 8 through 12, and middle school was grades 4 through 7. It was different, but the seniors were responsible for mentoring 8th and 9th graders as a part of their community service. It seemed like a good thing.

"You're new, right?" Marcus appeared beside me at my locker, leaning against the metal like he owned it. "I'm Marcus. Need someone to show you around? We are even supposed to help the 8th and 9th-grade students. You seem older. Are you still a freshman?"

I should have wondered why this boy was so interested in a thirteen-year-old eighth-grader, but I liked that he thought I was older. It felt nice to have a few acquaintances finally. I was starting to make at least one friend. I should have noticed how his compliments always came with subtle criticisms of everyone else in my life.

But I was so hungry for someone to see me, especially after I said I was in eighth grade and only 13. After years of being invisible in my own home, of making myself small so Daddy's rage would pass me by, here was this good-looking, popular boy telling me I was special.

It just seemed like a nice friendship, and I liked it. He even bought me special gifts and said this is just for me, because I was becoming such a sexy woman, and there must be a mistake about my age.

First came the attention texts that made me feel like the center of his universe. Then the isolation — "Your aunt and mom don't understand you like I do. Those other girls in your class are just jealous of you." Then the testing of boundaries began — a hand that lingered too long, a kiss that went further than I was ready for, always followed by "You're so mature for your age. Most girls couldn't handle this."

And the secrets. Always the secrets. Marcus was doing all the things you put in your book. I did read it last weekend, and everything was like you were writing about me.

He told me, "We have to be careful. People wouldn't understand what we have. I am only your mentor for everything strong women like you need. Don't talk to others about us because their jealousy would only try to break us up."

I was so desperate to be loved that I mistook control for care. I thought his jealousy meant I mattered. I thought his possessiveness was passion. I thought keeping secrets meant we were partners in something romantic and forbidden.

I didn't have words for what was really happening. Not then.

Now I do after reading the book you girls wrote and what I have learned in the group.

Grooming Manipulation, that thought was love and being special.

He knew exactly what he was doing. He saw the wounded girl in me — the one who'd learned to accept cruelty from the people who were supposed to protect me — and he exploited every crack in me.

The night it happened, I'd snuck out to meet him at the old barn on Route 12. I thought we were going to talk about prom, about our future. I was so naive.

He didn't hear me when I said no. Or maybe he heard and didn't care. He really hurt me, and I was crying and in pain. He took my chin in his one hand and said, "Now you are a real woman."

Afterward, I walked home in the dark, something broken inside me that had nothing to do with my body. I showered until the water went cold. I told myself it was my fault for sneaking out. For trusting him. For being stupid enough to believe someone like him could love someone like me.

I couldn't tell anyone. I was feeling so guilty.

Eight weeks ago, I woke up sick, and the calendar told me what the pregnancy test would confirm. I missed my period, and I had a friend get me a pregnancy test. It was positive, and that's when I told my mom.

"Marcus disappeared after that, but he even told me he loved me that day at the barn," as I continued to explain to Dr. Martinez, as my voice started cracking. "He said I was special. And I believed him because... because I needed to believe someone could love me. Now I see all that grooming crap from reading your book.

Dr. Martinez's eyes held mine, warm and unwavering. "Jalin, what Marcus did was not about love. It was about power and control. A seventeen-year-old pursuing a thirteen-year-old is his choice not really caring, but using manipulation and coercion — that's predatory behavior. The responsibility lies with him. Not with you."

"But I should have known—"

You were thirteen, and no, you were already fighting to survive family trauma, she said gently. "Predators recognize vulnerability and exploit it. That doesn't reflect your worth or intelligence; it reflects his choices. This is something he knew and then, he chose to ignore the moral compass in his head."

Imani reached over and took Jalin's hand. Angelina moved closer.

"You survived your father," Imani said quietly. "And you survived, Marcus You're still here."

Jalin looked at the other girls — each carrying their own invisible scars, their own stories of adults or near-adults who should have protected them but instead caused harm.

And for the first time since that night in the barn, Jalin let herself consider the possibility that maybe — just maybe — this wasn't her fault after all.

The girls came up and formed a large hugging circle, then repeated something new to Jalin.

I WAS GROOMED—IT WAS **NOT** MY FAULT.

I WAS GROOMED—IT WAS **NOT** MY FAULT.

Jalin added her voice, I WAS GROOMED—IT WAS **NOT** MY FAULT.

They all returned to their seats, but Rosa was clearly upset, and she didn't sit down.

"I don't know if I can keep doing this," Rosa said quietly, staring at her hands. "Every week, more girls. More stories. More predators, we can't stop. It's too big. We're just kids."

"We're not just kids," Angelina said, but her voice lacked its usual certainty. "We're—"

"Thirteen," Rosa interrupted. "We're thirteen. We're smart and brave and we've done amazing things, but Angelina—we're losing. There are too many of them and not enough of us."

Silence settled over the circle. Even Keisha, usually the first to fight, looked defeated.

Jalin, interrupted and said, "Wait. Wait. I am here. You are helping me. I still don't know what I will be able to do with my baby, but I know you guys won't abandon me. Right?"

They all responded with a yes or a nod. Dr. Martinez then asked Jalin to see her after the group to discuss being a mom at thirteen. "I know I can help you, Jalin."

The group ended, but would meet next week without Dr. Martinez, just as they had for over a year.

Author's Note: *This chapter introduces Jalin, a new member of the Threshold Group, whose story embodies the devastating intersection of family trauma and predatory grooming. Her journey from domestic violence survivor to grooming victim illustrates how predators deliberately target vulnerable young people already wounded by life circumstances. Jalin's story reveals how childhood trauma from witnessing and experiencing domestic violence created psychological vulnerabilities that Marcus exploited. Her father's abuse taught her to accept cruelty from those who claimed to care for her—a lesson the predator weaponized. The group's collective chanting—"I WAS GROOMED—IT WAS NOT MY FAULT"—creates a powerful ritual of responsibility reallocation. This communal affirmation serves multiple purposes.*

CHAPTER SEVEN

HEAVEN GETS A CALL

Angelina took a deep breath. Her heart pounded. She said it was time to try something that involved her angels, the ones you thought were my imagination, my hallucinations. Are all of you ready to call them? Nods went around the circle, except for Jalin, who was not sure what Angelina meant.

"I've always had help. Since I was six years old." She paused, ready to face her fear. "I see angels, but I don't know if anyone else will see them. Are you ready to try?"

Jalin looks a bit confused and says yes. "Me too," Jade added quickly. "I mean, I've never seen one. But I believe in them. I pray to them every night."

Same, Rosa said. "My abuela always said angels watch over us. I just... I never thought about actually seeing them."

Zara was crying softly. "I've prayed so hard for help. So hard. I wanted to believe someone was listening. I just never got an answer."

What about what we have now? What about finding some adults who take big risks to help us? That might be your prayers being answered," Angelina responded.

Keisha looked uncomfortable. "I don't know about all that. I mean, I'm not saying you're lying, Angelina. But I've never seen anything that made me think angels are real."

Angelina nodded. "That's fair. And I've asked them why they don't get involved more. They say they can't interfere with human free will—people have to make their own choices. But they CAN help when we ask. When we invite them. When we open ourselves to receiving help."

So ask them," Keisha said, still skeptical but desperate enough to try anything. "If they're real, if they can help—ask them to come help us."

Maya stood up and looked at everyone. "Don't all of you believe in science? How can you honestly think there are angels running around like the "Men-in-Black?"" She sat back down and glanced at the floor. "Look, this floor is real. That window is real. Angels are not real. Do you all understand? Sorry, Angelina, I just can't get there."

Maya, I care about you, and you don't have to believe anything that makes you uncomfortable. Would you like to come with us, or would you rather go home?

"I really am sorry," Maya said with pain in her voice. "I need to stick to what I believe, and angels are not real. I guess I'll go home. I'll be here next Friday for the group. I won't make fun of you if you don't see any. Enjoy."

"Well, you asked if I had already talked to the angels about them coming tonight at midnight. I already did," Angelina said. "Two of them—Raphael and Michael—said they'd come tonight. To meet all of you. To offer help."

"When?" Jade asked, glancing around nervously as if angels might appear from her closet.

Soon. But first, I need to teach you something. They can't appear to people who are completely closed off, who are vibrating at... at a lower frequency. She struggled to find the right words. "We need to prepare ourselves. Open ourselves. I know this frequency thing is weird, but every living thing has a frequency. We all vibrate because the stuff that makes us is living cells that are constantly moving. It creates a frequency—a vibration. The problem occurs when we are full of fear, anger, confusion, depression, or even jealousy; we vibrate at a low frequency. We need to practice raising our frequency. Now you can see why I was feeling fearful about telling you all this. But my own fear needs to be raised as well.

"How?" Jade leaned forward eagerly.

Breathing. Heart-centered breathing. It sounds simple, but it's powerful," Angelina demonstrated, placing her right hand over her heart and her left hand on her belly. "One hand on your heart—this connects you to love, to your emotional center. One hand on your belly—this keeps you grounded and helps you breathe deeply. Come back at midnight. Jade, can you let us in through the garage side door? It is right by your room, and we can get in quietly.

"Not a problem, Midnight. See you tonight. Jalin, you and Rosa should stay here tonight. Rosa, ask your mom if you can have one more girl sleep over. She might be happy about that if her boyfriend is over. No attention split away from her own needs." Rosa, set the stage for three of them to be there with Zara already being a regular at the house by now.

The girls mimicked her position, hands on their hearts and bellies. Keisha started to laugh, "can you imagine the kids at school see us like this? OK, I'm doing it."

Now breathe. Take deep breaths for a count of 5 through your nose. It makes the inhale deeper. Now let out the air through your nose for a count of 5. These are much deeper than usual. Make sure your belly goes out when you breathe—belly breaths will move your belly hand up and down. Feel your heart under your other hand. Imagine you're breathing in light, breathing out fear. Breathing in hope, breathing out despair. Let's do this together.

They breathed together. Seven girls in a circle, breathing in synchrony, hands on hearts and bellies. This was the start. The start of something very new, very different, very confusing.

The room began to feel different. Warmer, somehow. The air seemed to shimmer.

"Keep breathing," Angelina whispered. "And if you feel scared when they appear, remember—fear and love can't exist in the same place. Choose love. Choose openness. Choose to receive help."

The air continued to shimmer, and then—

They appeared.

Two figures made of light stood in the center of the circle. Not solid, but not transparent either. They looked vaguely humanoid—tall, with wings that weren't quite wings, more like the space around them rippled with energy.

One radiated green-gold light that felt like healing. The other blazed with blue-white fire that felt like protection.

Jalin gasped. Keisha's eyes went wide. Even those who believed had never expected actually to see this, whatever they were.

The green-gold figure spoke first, and the voice came from everywhere and nowhere, gentle as summer rain:

I am Raphael. I have been called the Healer. Thank you for inviting us into your presence.

The blue-white figure followed, voice like distant thunder, powerful but not frightening:

I am Michael. I have been called the Protector. We honor your courage in asking for help.

"Holy shit," Keisha whispered, then clapped her hand over her mouth. "Sorry. Sorry. I just—you're real. You're actually real."

Raphael's light seemed to pulse with what might have been amusement. *We are as real as you allow us to be. Belief opens doors. Your invitation allows us to enter.*

"Can you help us?" Zara asked, tears streaming down her face. "Please. We've tried everything. We're drowning in this. There are too many predators, too many girls being hurt, and we're just—we're just kids and we don't know what else to do."

Michael's blue-white fire intensified. *We can help. But you have done so much for each other and some of your school friends. When we help you, we also need you to do something difficult from you. When we tell you, you might get confused about what we mean, so listen closely.*

"Anything," Jade said immediately. "We'll do anything."

Do not promise before you hear the terms, Raphael cautioned gently. *Always be careful and get all the information before you commit. What we offer is powerful, but the cost is high. Not in pain or sacrifice in the usual sense. The cost is spiritual growth beyond what thirteen-year-olds typically achieve.*

"Explain," Angelina said.

Michael spoke: *We can provide you with what you might call... human support people that help us. We call them Starseeds who travel around like real people all over the earth, and will accompany you when you confront your abusers. They will appear as men in dark suits—a form humans find authoritative, based on your cultural references to films called 'The Matrix' and 'Men in Black.' These are trusted men who help use deal with humans who are not able to understand a warning. They will show up for you, but it may take a day if they are not in your immediate area. Does this imagery resonate with you?*

Several girls nodded, almost smiling despite the gravity of the moment.

These Starseeds will ensure you are heard, Michael continued. They will play your recordings with you. They will deliver warnings that cannot be ignored. When they tell a predator that consequences will follow if abuse continues, those consequences will manifest. Things will make their lives miserable, and opportunities will close. Life will begin to crumble in ways that feel coincidental but are not. Then if anything continues, the tapes will be sent out.

"That sounds perfect," Keisha said. "When do we start?"

When you meet the condition, Raphael said. *And this is the difficult part. You must forgive.*

The word hit hard like a bomb.

"Forgive?" Zara's voice was sharp with anger. "Forgive my father for raping me? Forgive—no. No. I can't. I won't."

Raphael quickly clarified that we are not asking you to forgive your father's actions. *Those actions warrant consequences. Justice must be served. Men who harm children need to face both earthly and spiritual accountability.*

What we ask, Michael added, is that you forgive the soul that was lost. The spirit that was once innocent, that chose the dark path, and that became something terrible. Forgive that soul's lostness without excusing what it did in that person.

"I don't understand the difference," Imani said, confusedly.

Raphael's green-gold light settled over her like a warm blanket. *You can say: 'I hate what you did. I will never excuse your actions. You deserve consequences and I will ensure you face them. But I release my hatred of your soul. I forgive the part of you that was once a child, that once had the potential for goodness, that got corrupted and lost. I forgive your soul for losing its way, even as I demand justice for your actions.'*

"That's..." Jade struggled for words. "That's really hard."

Michael acknowledged that t*his is the hardest work humans can do. It is what your teacher Jesus meant when he said to love your enemies. Not to excuse them. Not to allow them to continue harming. But to refuse to let hatred poison your own soul.*

"What if I can't?" Zara asked, still angry but also desperate. "What if I try and I just... can't stop hating him? He's my father. He was supposed to protect me, and instead he—" Her voice broke.

Raphael moved closer to her (or the light did, shifting in that direction). *Then you are human, and that is acceptable. Forgiveness is not a single act but a journey. You may walk that path for years. But if you are willing to try—if you can say 'I want to forgive the lost soul even though I cannot yet'—that willingness opens the door.*

Hatred, Michael added, *lowers your frequency. It makes you vibrate at the same level as those who harmed you. Forgiveness—of the soul, not the actions—raises your frequency to match the divine. This is how you grow beyond what was done to you. This is how you reclaim your power.*

Imani spoke up: "This is what Jesus taught. Forgive seventy times seven, isn't it? But I always thought that meant letting people hurt you over and over. This is different. This is... forgive the person but still stop the harm."

Exactly, Imani, **Raphael confirmed.** *The old law was 'an eye for an eye.' Your teacher brought a new message from his Father-God: forgiveness paired with boundaries. Love paired with consequences. You can forgive* a soul and still call the police. You can release hatred and still testify in court. You can refuse to let darkness consume your heart while still fighting darkness in the world.

And if we can do this?" Angelina asked. "If we can learn to forgive the souls while demanding justice for their actions—then do we get the men in dark suits? The escorts?"

You get more than that, Michael said. *You have a direct line to divine help. Whenever you need protection, support, or intervention, you meditate, breathe as Angelina taught you, and ask with an open heart—help comes to you. If you need the 'men-in-black,' they will arrive. The promise is old and unchanging: 'Ask and it shall be given unto you. Seek and ye shall find. Knock and the door shall be opened.' Most adults, even those who go to church, don't believe this is real, but it is.*

But you must ask, Raphael emphasized. *You need to raise your vibration above those that are hurting you, then ask. So many humans believe in us but never ask for help. They pray in desperation but don't truly expect an answer. They go to churches and temples but treat the divine as distant, unavailable. We are always here. We have always been here. Waiting to be invited. Waiting for you to raise your frequency so you can hear the divine talk back to you in love. That is His only frequency. LOVE.*

Maya walked in so quietly that no one heard her sit next to Rosa. Then, she spoke with her very practical voice, even in the presence of what she was seeing: "So we meditate, we ask, and men in dark suits appear to help us confront our abusers?"

Hi Maya, I'm so happy you decided to join us. Michael and I know you've thought about this in terms of physics and science, and we understand that. What's ahead for you will be very influential. When you're older, you'll introduce Quantum Physics to young people like yourself. You will be landing space stations on Mars someday. Eventually, you'll see that the most advanced physics includes beings from other worlds—including angels. Thank you for coming, and you are almost correct in your question.

"And these men will be... what, angels in disguise?" Maya asked.

Consider them as extensions of the divine that come from your time, taking a form your culture acknowledges as authoritative. They will speak with your voice—delivering the messages you choose—yet with weight and power that cannot be ignored or dismissed. They truly exist on earth, and their souls continuously return to assist you.

"And we have to forgive the souls of the men who hurt us," Maya again added her deep distress over what was happening.

You must try to start the journey of forgiveness. It's not about achieving complete forgiveness right away — that might take years — but about setting your intention toward it. Remember, it is their lost soul you are forgiving, not the person's actions.

The eight girls looked at each other. A silent conversation passed between them, the kind only people who've survived together can have.

Finally, Zara spoke: "I'll try. I don't know if I can. But I'll try. Because if there's a chance this works, if there's a chance my father faces consequences and I don't have to hate him so much it eats me alive... I'll try."

One by one, the others agreed.

"We'll try."

"I'll try."

"Okay. Yes. I'll try."

That is all we ask, Raphael said, and the warmth of his words felt like being held by a parent who actually loved you. *Your willingness opens the door. Now, place your hands back on your hearts and bellies. Breathe deeply. And understand: You are not children fighting adult battles. You are divine beings remembering your power. You are goddess energy in thirteen-year-old bodies. You carry within you the same creative force that made stars and souls. That is why we bow to you. That is why we serve you when invited."*

And, despite how impossible it seemed, the two beings of light bowed, lowering themselves in respect to the eight thirteen-year-old girls sitting in a circle on the bedroom floor.

You are worthy, Michael said. *You have always been worthy. The darkness tried to convince you otherwise. But your beauty, your power, your divine nature—these cannot be stolen by predators. They can only be forgotten. We are here to help you remember.*

Call on us, Raphael added. *Meditate, ask, and we send assistance. You will never be abandoned. This is the promise of God to the divine feminine: You are seen. You are loved. You are protected when you ask.*

The light began to fade, the figures dissolving like mist in sunlight.

One more thing, Michael's voice emerged from the fading brightness. *Do not tell everyone about us. Those who can hear will hear, and those who cannot will dismiss or mock, which will only cause doubt in your hearts. Guard this knowledge carefully. Use it wisely. Trust it fully. It's amazing how many people go to worship God every week and read stories like the power of a mustard seed that can move mountains, but they don't believe and are not willing to forgive the soul that was lost.*

And they were gone.

Eight girls sat in silence, hands still on hearts and bellies, tears streaming down most of their faces.

"Did that just happen?" Maya whispered.

"Yes," seven voices answered simultaneously.

Three days had passed, and Rosa knew Zara was staying at Angelina's home for a couple of weeks. She actually enjoyed Zara being their because this kept her mother's boyfriend away. But she needed to stand up to him at some point. She stood in her bedroom, her mother's boyfriend due home any minute. She was terrified but determined.

For three days, she'd been practicing. Breathing with hands on heart and belly. Trying to forgive—not what he'd done, never what he'd done, but the soul that had become so twisted it could hurt a child.

It was hard. The hardest thing she'd ever attempted. Every time she thought she'd managed it, rage would flood back. "He's a monster. He deserves to suffer, and probably heard Zara was leaving for a few weeks."

But then she'd remember Raphael's words: *Hatred lowers your frequency. Forgiveness raises it.*

And she'd breathe and try again. "I forgive your lost soul. I hate your actions. I forgive your lost soul. I demand consequences. I forgive your lost soul. I will not be poisoned by hating you."

She heard his car in the driveway.

Her mother was working the night shift at the hospital. Rosa would be alone with him for the next three hours.

He'd escalated over the past month. The touching became more frequent and invasive. Last week, he'd cornered her in the kitchen, his hands on her hips, saying things that made her skin crawl. She pushed away, but he laughed. "You're being dramatic. I'm just being affectionate."

Tonight, he'd come to her room. She knew it with unshakable certainty. Tonight, he'd try to go further than he ever had.

But tonight, she received help.

The front door swung open. His voice called up the stairs: "Rosa? You home?"

In my room," she called back, her voice steadier than she felt.

She sat on her bed, placed her hands on her heart and belly, and began to breathe—deeper than normal and slower. She felt her heart beating under her palm and her belly rising and falling.

"Please," she thought, directing the word to Raphael, Michael, and the divine force they represented. "Please send help. I need protection. I need to be heard. I need him to stop."

Footsteps on the stairs.

Rosa's bedroom door swung open without knocking. Never asked for permission, never knocked—he just opened her door like he owned every space in the house, including hers.

"Hey there," he said, smiling that smile that used to seem friendly but now looked predatory. "Thought maybe we could hang out. Watch a movie together. You seemed stressed lately—thought you could use some company."

"I don't want company," Rosa said clearly. Her phone was recording in her pocket, as it always was now. "I want you to leave my room," she added as she walked down the stairs to the living room with him right behind her, then sat on the couch.

Now don't act like that. I'm only trying to be nice—

He stood up and took her hand,

And then he froze.

The room's atmosphere shifted. Pressure changed. The temperature dropped.

Two men entered the house, looked at Rosa, and then stood between Rosa and the predator.

They wore dark suits — perfectly tailored and subtly stylish. Dark glasses, even indoors. They appeared to be in their thirties, ethnically ambiguous, with faces that were both distinctive and forgettable. You could look directly at them and not be able to describe their faces five minutes later.

But they radiated authority—the kind that makes you straighten your spine, shut your mouth, sit down and listen.

"What the—" the predator stumbled backward unto the sofa. "Who are you? How did you get in here?"

The men didn't respond to him; they turned to Rosa.

"Ms. Rosa," one of them said, his voice professionally neutral but carrying significant weight. "Are you ready to deliver your message?"

Rosa stood on shaky legs. She had prepared what she wanted to say and rehearsed it a dozen times. Now, with these impossible beings standing guard, she found her voice.

"You need to listen," she told her mother's boyfriend. "And you're going to listen because you don't have a choice anymore."

She pulled out her phone, opened the recording app with weeks of saved files, chose one from two weeks ago, and pressed play.

His voice echoed through the speaker: "You're getting so beautiful, Rosa. So grown up. Your mother doesn't appreciate what a woman you're becoming. But I do. I notice everything..."

Then another recording. His hands on her, his heavy breathing, her saying "Stop" and him saying "Come on, don't be uptight. I'm just showing you affection..."

Recording after recording. His voice. His words. Undeniable proof.

His face had gone pale. "Rosa, you can't—those are private—"

"Nothing was private," Rosa said, anger fueling her strength. "You made everything no longer private when you entered my room, touched me without asking, and said things no adult should say to a child."

One of the dark-suited men said, "Mr. Hernandez. You will listen without interrupting."

The predator's mouth snapped shut, not because he chose to stay quiet, but because he physically couldn't speak. His eyes widened with panic.

"Better listen," the man said. "Ms. Rosa has conditions. You will listen. You will comply. Or you'll find that life has a way of unraveling for men who prey on children."

Rosa took a shaky breath. "These are my terms. One: You move out of this house. Today. Now. You pack a bag, leave, and never come back. Two: You get therapy. Real therapy, with someone who specializes in sexual offending. I have a list of names." She held up a paper prepared by the Sweet Seven—a list from Dr. Martinez. "You choose one and start going, or what happens next is worse. Three: You never contact me again. Not a text, an email, a phone call, or showing up at my school. Never. Four: You tell my mother you're leaving because you're not healthy for this family. Not because I accused you—because YOU chose to leave. If you blame me or make her doubt me, what happens next is worse."

"What comes next?" he managed to choke out.

The second man in a dark suit smiled. It wasn't a friendly smile. "You will be taken in with the deportations that are happening. No court. No warrant. Just deportation because you'll be in the wrong place at the wrong time. More will happen if you come back."

"And if you reoffend," the first man added, "if you target another child, anywhere, ever—we return. Not to talk. To ensure consequences far more severe than uncomfortable conversations and deportations. Do you understand?"

The predator nodded, terrified.

"Speak," the man commanded, and suddenly he could.

"I understand," he gasped. "I'll go. I'll get help. I won't contact her. I'll tell Rosa's mother I need to leave."

Good,

He stumbled out of the room, moving as if in a nightmare.

The two men looked at Rosa, and their expressions softened.

"You were very brave," one said.

"Will he really do it?" Rosa asked. "Will he actually leave and get help?"

"Compliance is not guaranteed," the man admitted. "Free will remains. But the consequences we described will manifest if he fails to comply. And fear is a powerful motivator. Most men, when confronted with the certainty of consequences, choose the path of least resistance."

"And my mom?"

She will believe what he says. Whether she searches for the deeper truth is her decision. But you are safer now than you were an hour ago.

"Thank you," Rosa whispered.

"Thank Raphael and Michael," the second man said. "Thank the divine force that heard your prayer. Thank yourself for having the courage to ask for help and demand better."

"And thank your sisters," the first man added. "The Sweet Seven-plus. You do not fight alone."

They simply slipped out of the room so smoothly she couldn't track their movement. Either way, one moment they were there, and the next she was alone.

Rosa sat on her bed, shaking with adrenaline, relief, and disbelief at what had just happened.

She grabbed her phone and sent a message to the group chat:

Rosa told the group, "It worked. Oh my god, it worked. Two men in dark suits appeared. He's packing right now. He's leaving. IT WORKED."

The responses came immediately:

"WHAT?" Jade blurted out.

Angelina smiled and said, "I knew they'd come. I knew it." Zara said, "Oh, I should have been there, I'm sorry."

"No fucking way" was all Kesha could say with her rougher edges that sometimes shocked the other girls..

Rosa told Zara, "No, no, I am glad I could do this. It was time."

Rosa added smile after smile emoji to the message, "I'm okay. I'm better than okay. I'm FREE."

Imani looked at everyone with amazement, "I … I just didn't think we could get that kind of help." Jade looked straight at Imani, with a look of confused joy, "We both said we pray to God all the time, and we just didn't really believe our own prayers."

Angelina needed to contribute more to that confusing connection happening, "Do you remember what we have to do to raise our own frequency to that of the divine? Was forgiveness ever in your thoughts? Would you have ever considered the need to forgive, given the pain and anger we have experienced? I don't think I would have ever considered that myself."

"Yes," Rosa said as she was calming down, "I forgive his lost soul. But he'd better run."

The Sweet Seven-Plus gathered in Jade's bedroom the next Friday.

So much had changed in just seven days.

Rosa's mother's boyfriend had moved out that same night. Told her mother he needed to work on himself, that he wasn't healthy for the family. Her mother was sad but accepting and Rosa was safe.

Since then, four more girls have called on the angels' help. Four more visits from men in dark suits. Four more predators faced evidence and consequences.

Not everyone cooperated right away. One person tried to call the bluff, laughed, and said nothing would happen. The next day, that man's car broke down. Then his direct deposit mysteriously rerouted. After that, his boss received an anonymous package of evidence. He called the girl he'd been grooming, terrified, asking what he needed to do to make it stop. She told him: therapy, distance, forever.

He agreed.

Tonight, the girls sat in a bedroom, not to ask for more help but to give thanks.

They held hands at first and then sat. With their hands on their hearts and bellies in the pattern Angelina had shown them, they all took deep breaths.

"Raphael, Michael," Angelina said softly while sitting with the other girls. "We asked for help, and you answered. We asked for protection, and you provided it. We asked for our voices to be heard, and you made sure they were. We don't have words big enough to thank you."

The air shimmered, and this time all eight of them could see it clearly. The angels appeared, but in a different way—less solid, more like impressions of light, as if they were there but not fully present.

You don't need to thank us, Raphael's voice came like a warm wind. *You did the work. You found courage. You spoke your truth. We simply amplified what was already within you. You may not remember, but the Holy Spirit came directly from God and can be in every person at once. That is the part of God that works with all people—if they are listening.*

Michael added, *The divine feminine energy that has been suppressed for thousands of years—is returning to life in girls like you. For that, we thank you.*

"But we couldn't have done it without you," Jade said. "Without the men in dark suits, without knowing you were real and listening—"

You might believe that, but imagine if it is not true? Raphael said softly. *We do not come from outside. We emerge from the divine spark within you. When you ask for help, you are not summoning something external—you're activating the Holy Spirit within you. Your own connection to Source. Your own goddess nature has been activated. Now you have learned the need to raise your frequency and to understand Jesus's message of 'love your enemy.'*

That sounds like a metaphor," Maya said, still skeptical. "Are you saying you're real or are we just tapping into our own power?"

Both, Michael said, with a hint of humor in his tone. We are as real as the love you feel for each other. As real as the courage you've shown. Reality is more complex than humans usually realize. We exist. You exist. The divine exists in, through, and between all of it. The question of 'where do you end and we begin' does not have a simple answer.

"So when we meditate and call for help," Angelina asked, "and the men in dark suits appear—are those angels? Or are they manifestations of our own power? Or both?"

Yes, both angels said at the same time, and the laughter in their voices sounded like music.

"That's not an answer," Keisha mumbled just loud enough.

It is the only honest answer, Raphael said. You want clear categories: supernatural or natural, external or internal, real or imagined. But we operate in the space between categories. We are both the help you call for and the power you access within yourselves. We are both the divine reaching down and the divine within you reaching up. The meeting point is what creates miracles—or brings Men in Black, who we call Starseeds.

"Will you always come when we ask?" Keisha's voice was softer than usual, more vulnerable. "Promise you won't leave us? Oh wait, I guess I can't leave myself, can I? This is very confusing for me."

We promise you are never truly abandoned, Michael said, and the weight of that promise felt like an oath written in starlight. As long as you remember to ask, as long as you keep your willingness to forgive what can be forgiven while demanding justice for actions, we are with you. Not always visible. Not always in forms you can see or touch. But present. Always.

You are goddess energy in thirteen-year-old bodies, Raphael said, and his light seemed to enfold all eight girls in warmth. You are sacred feminine power in human form. You are a beauty that predators try to possess but cannot, because beauty cannot be owned. You are a strength that the world tries to suppress but cannot, because truth always rises. You are loved beyond measure, protected beyond sight, guided beyond knowing.

Walk in that truth, Michael added. *Walk knowing you carry divinity within you. Not arrogantly—humility is strength. But knowing your worth, your power, your connection to Source--God. When men try to diminish you, remember you are divine. When systems fail you, remember you have access to power beyond systems. When the world tells you that you're just children, just girls, just victims—remember you are goddesses who have talked with angels.*

The light started to fade once more, as the angels disappeared into the night air.

One final gift, Raphael's voice came from the fading light. *Look at each other. Really look. See the light that radiates from each of you. See the divine spark. See the goddess's power. You are mirrors for each other of what is sacred, powerful, and beautiful. Never forget what you see in this moment.*

And for just a moment, just an instant, the eight girls saw it—the light that surrounded each of them, the radiance that's not about physical beauty but about the soul. They viewed themselves as the angels saw them: divine beings living human lives, sacred feminine energy made real, goddesses in the act of remembering their power.

Then the vision faded, and just eight thirteen-year-old girls were standing in a field at midnight.

But they weren't just ordinary.

They were the Sweet Seven-Plus,

They were survivors who had turned into warriors.

They were girls who had learned to pray to heaven and discovered that heaven answered.

They marked the start of something that would spread—to other schools, other cities, and other girls who needed to know they weren't powerless, that they could fight back, and that they were never abandoned.

"So," Maya said, breaking the reverent silence with her usual practicality. "Same time next week?"

Jalin was now part of the group and still reeling from everything that had happened. She could only say, "I was groomed, It is not my fault," as the other girls cheered.

They all laughed, tension easing into the night air. Then Jalin looked at her belly, "Sisters, I am still in need of some help here. Do you see this belly? It is getting big, and I have a much harder time getting around. Can you all help me?"

The question lingered in the air like golf-ball-sized hail ready to drop from the clouds. They looked—they all looked at her with curious wonder and empathetic eyes.

Same time next week," Angelina confirmed. " But this time we need to be here for Jalin. She needs us to help her with everything: school work, getting around. decisions to be made, and anything else she is going through. I think this would be a good time to ask Dr. Martinez to visit our group. I think we can stay focused on our work, AND our support for our sister.

"Are we really doing all this," Jade commented with some concern. "We ARE middle schoolers. But, we just happen to be goddesses. I guess that means we can do all this when we need to."

"Very Raphael of you," Maya teased.

The following Friday, they strolled toward Jade's apartment, arms linked and supporting each other as they always did. Zara spoke softly: "I forgave him today. My father. Not what he did—I'll never forgive that. But I forgave his soul. I said it out loud, alone in my room, and something... shifted. I still want consequences for him. I still think he should be in jail. But I don't hate him with that burning, consuming hatred anymore. It's like... I put down a weight I didn't realize I was carrying."

"That's beautiful," Angelina said, squeezing her hand.

"It's hard," Zara continued. "It's the hardest thing I've ever done. Harder than surviving the abuse. Harder than leaving home. But I think... I think it's working. I think I'm getting free. Actually free, not just physically safe but spiritually free."

"That's what the angels meant," Angelina said softly. "About raising our frequency. About matching divine energy. We can't be consumed by hatred and also be filled with goddess power. There's no room for both."

So we choose goddess power," Maya said. "We choose divine frequency. We choose to forgive lost souls while still demanding justice for evil actions.

Jade added, "We choose to be both merciful and fierce."

Both forgiving and uncompromising," Angelina continued.

Both compassionate and dangerous to predators," Keisha finished.

Maya, walking slightly ahead, turned back to look at her sisters. "You know what we are? We're the generation that breaks the curse. For thousands of years, thirteen-year-old girls disappeared. But we're still here. Visible. Powerful. Protected by angels and armed with truth. We're the ones who change what thirteen means."

They reached the apartment complex and paused before going inside. Now it's time to help Jalin.

Eight girls, thirteen years old, standing under streetlights in Liberty City at midnight. Girls who should have been victims. Girls who'd been targeted by predators who thought they were easy prey.

But these girls had learned to call on their inner strength within and from above.

And the universe answered.

"Thank you," Angelina whispered to the night sky, to the angels she couldn't see but knew were listening. "Thank you for teaching us we're never alone. Thank you for showing us our power. Thank you for protecting us when we remember to ask for protection."

Jalin quietly whispered loudly enough for everyone to hear, as she looked up at the sky. "Raphael, would you please join us because I need your loving support. The girls are ready. I am ready. And it is time to make some decisions. I accept your guidance tonight."

A warm breeze drifted through the complex, even though the night had been completely still just a moment earlier.

This time, the angels didn't respond with words.

But the breeze felt like a blessing and an answer for Jalin.

Like a promise kept.

Like love from unseen sources. They were finally heading to Jade's for the big sleepover, something they had talked about but hadn't done until today. "First, we hear what Jalin needs, and then we have popcorn and drinks," Jade said, opening her door at the same time.

The Sweet Seven-Plus went inside, exhausted yet exhilarated, ready to work for a few more hours if needed, and then sleep and dream of fields bathed in light and children playing without fear.

Tomorrow, they'll wake up still thirteen, still caught in harmful cycles. Still fighting systems that fail them. Still saving other girls, one effort at a time, and one getting ready to be a m----. "You are going to be a mom," Imani told Jalin. "That is a miracle all by itself."

They felt they could do all of this knowing they were divine. They felt protected. They embodied goddess energy in thirteen-year-old bodies.

And they were never, ever abandoned. "Jalin, I am here for you. Did you call me?" a voice came from the corner of the bedroom with a blucish light in the middle.

END Of CHAPTER SEVEN

Author's Note: This chapter introduces the spiritual and supernatural intervention the girls need while maintaining a focus on realistic trauma responses. The angels don't fix everything—they empower the girls to resolve their own issues. Requiring forgiveness of souls while demanding justice for actions is a nuanced spiritual lesson that recognizes the complexity of healing from abuse. The "men in dark suits" provide both practical support (confronting predators with authority) and uphold the girls' agency (by delivering their messages and setting boundaries). This chapter transitions the story from a realistic drama about abuse to a broader, mythological narrative about the divine feminine power reclaiming itself. The breathing and meditation techniques are real and usable by actual readers, making this chapter both a story and a practical guide for spiritual growth, while knowing they will all need to support Jalin's decision about the baby.

Chapter Eight

GIFT RECEIVED AND GIFT GIVEN

Challenging, but Purposeful Decisions

It was early May, and several of the girls had already turned fourteen. They still meet weekly, but Jalin had been meeting with Dr. Martinez separately as well. They had made a final decision to give the baby up for an open adoption. This would allow Jalin to stay involved in the baby's life, while the adoptive parents would be the official parents.

The conference room at Dr. Martinez's office had been transformed. Gone were the usual sterile chairs arranged in clinical rows. Instead, soft couches formed a circle, and someone—probably Dr. Martinez herself— had brought in floor pillows in jewel tones that caught the late afternoon sun streaming through the windows. A table along the wall held sparkling water, juice boxes (a knowing nod to their not-so-distant childhood), and a platter of homemade-looking cookies.

Angelina arrived first, as usual. Punctuality was her shield against chaos, and tonight felt like it might break open into something too large for any of them to handle alone.

Dr. Martinez greeted her at the door, her dark eyes warm yet scrutinizing. "How are you feeling about tonight?"

"I don't know," Angelina admitted. "Nervous? For Jalin. This feels huge."

"It is huge," Dr. Martinez agreed. "Jalin is doing something incredibly brave. And she wanted all of you here to witness it, to meet the people who will raise her son. That tells me everything I need to know about what you girls mean to each other."

The others arrived in a wave: Maya and Imani together, Jade with Zara, Keisha, Rosa, and finally Jalin herself, eight months pregnant and moving with the careful deliberation of someone carrying precious cargo. Her mother had driven her but waited in the parking lot—Jalin had asked for this time with just her sisters.

They immediately surrounded her, this girl who was becoming a mother without actually becoming one, and Angelina watched Jalin's face soften into something like peace. Here, among them, she could just be Jalin. Not a statistic. Not a cautionary tale. Not a pregnant teen.

Just Jalin.

"They're really nice," Jalin said, settling onto a couch with the kind of groan that comes from carrying extra weight in front. "Mark and Loral. I've met with them three times now. They're... they're going to be good parents."

"Tell us about them," Imani urged, pulling out her ever-present sketchbook.

Jalin's face softened. "Loral works as a children's librarian. Can you imagine? My baby—their baby—is going to grow up surrounded by books. And Mark, he's a marine biologist. Studies sea turtles. He showed me pictures of him tagging them on the beach at sunrise." She paused, her hand unconsciously moving to her belly. "They're the kind of people who would have been my baby's parents anyway, you know? If the universe worked right. If I was thirty instead of just turning fourteen. Maybe I would have met just the right guy as well and then..."

She didn't finish. Didn't need to. They all knew what Marcus had been— what he'd taken from her, what he'd left behind.

Dr. Martinez checked her watch. "They should arrive in about ten minutes. Is there anything you want to discuss before the Brooks arrive?"

"The open adoption thing," Keisha said. "Can you explain how that works? Because I'm still wrapping my head around it."

Dr. Martinez nodded, slipping into her teacher mode with practiced ease. "In a traditional closed adoption, the birth mother has no contact with the child after placement. The records are sealed. Everyone moves on separately. But Jalin wanted something different—she wanted to be part of her son's life, just not as his mother. An open adoption allows for that."

"So I can see him," Jalin explained, her voice growing stronger. "Not all the time—Mark and Loral are his parents, and they make all the decisions about his life. But we've agreed on visits. Maybe once a month at first, with pictures and updates in between. When he's old enough, they'll tell him about me. About us. About where he came from."

"Like a big sister," Rosa said softly.

"Exactly like a big sister." Jalin's eyes shimmered. "I can't be his mom. I'm not ready for that. I'm still a kid myself. But I can love him from a distance. I can watch him grow up with parents who chose him, who wanted him desperately, who can give him everything I can't."

"That's not giving up," Maya said fiercely. "That's love in its purest form—its giving a precious gift after receiving something for myself as well."

The door chimed, and Dr. Martinez rose. "That's them."

Mark and Loral Brooks entered the room with the tentative energy of people who knew they were being judged. It felt like their entire future depended on the opinions of eight teenage girls.

Mark was tall and sun-weathered, with smile lines around his eyes and hands that looked at ease holding both babies and sea creatures. Loral was petite, with auburn hair pulled back in a practical ponytail and an open, expressive face that couldn't hide her emotions.

They were young—twenty-eight and twenty-five—but carried themselves with a gravitas that revealed pain endured, dreams put on hold, and hope cautiously rebuilt.

"Hi," Loral said, her voice soft but steady. "Thank you for having us. Jalin has told us so much about all of you."

The Sweet Seven—now eight with Jalin's presence—aligned themselves like a jury, protective and evaluating. Angelina felt the weight of it—this moment when they would collectively decide if these strangers were worthy of their sister's child, or at least that was what they believed their role to be.

Mark and Loral sat, while Dr. Martinez facilitated the introductions. Names, ages, and small details that create bridges between strangers.

Jalin wanted you to meet us," Loral started, "because you're her family. The real kind, the chosen kind. And we want you to know that we understand what a gift she's giving us. We don't take it lightly.

"Tell them," Jalin prompted gently. "Tell them about the accident."

Loral's hand moved unconsciously to her abdomen, mirroring Jalin's gesture. "Two years ago, Mark and I were in a car accident. A drunk driver ran a red light. Mark was mostly okay—broken arm, concussion. But I had internal injuries. They saved my life, but..." Her voice wavered. "They couldn't save my ability to have children. The damage was too extensive."

"We grieved," Mark continued, taking his wife's hand. "For a long time, we grieved. We'd always wanted kids. It was part of our plan, our future. Suddenly, that future was gone."

But then we started learning about adoption," Loral said, her voice growing stronger. "And we realized that maybe this was always meant to be our path. That maybe the family we were supposed to have was waiting for us in a different way.

Imani leaned forward. "Have you told your families? About adopting Jalin's baby?"

"Our families are thrilled," Mark said. "My parents are already buying out every baby store in Miami. Loral's mom has knitted enough blankets to cover a small army of babies."

They know about me?" Jalin asked. "About... everything?"

They know you're almost fourteen," Loral said softly. "They realize you were hurt by someone who should have been your mentor. They see you're making an incredibly mature decision. And they can't wait to tell their grandson, when he's old enough to understand, about the courageous young woman who loved him enough to choose this life for him, even when it was difficult.

Angelina watched Jalin's face crumple and then smooth out, saw her cry and laugh at the same time, a moment that only happens when grief and joy mix.

"Can you tell us about the open adoption part?" Keisha asked, her protector instincts engaged and curious. "How will that actually work?"

Mark pulled out a folder—organized and prepared. "We've created a schedule with Dr. Martinez's help. For the first six months, we'll send photos and updates weekly. Jalin can visit once a month, or more if everyone feels comfortable. As he gets older, we'll adjust based on what's healthiest for him."

"We live in Miami," Loral added. "That's about four hours from here. But we're planning to spend time in this area regularly. Mark's research takes him to the Keys, and we pass right through Liberty City. We want him to know this place, to know his birth mom—his first family."

"First family," Maya repeated, trying out the words.

"You are his family, too," Loral said, looking at each of them in turn. "All of you. Jalin has shared stories—about your bedroom meetings, your secrets, your fierce loyalty to each other. This baby is coming into the world with eight guardian angels. We're honored that you're willing to be part of his life."

Mark looked down then up toward the ceiling. "We also have a strange story to tell you. We were struggling with what to do after hearing we could not have children. For almost two years, we mourned this inability to have kids, and then one Friday evening—maybe it was midnight—a voice entered our room. The voice was kind. He said his name was Raphael, and he had a message for us. He said there was a special girl who was too young to be a mom, but she was going to have a beautiful boy who needed a home like ours. If we were ready to be parents, he would help the girl find her way to us — especially if we could be accepting of an open adoption."

We couldn't believe what we heard. The voice was so clear, caring for us and seemingly for the girl as well. We called the adoption agency the next day, and that was when Jalin had already contacted them too," Loral explained. "Then, after our second meeting, Jalin said it was Friday night at midnight when all of you were meeting, and she asked 'Raphael,' her angel, to help her. And he did.

The seven girls looked at Jalin immediately and smiled with affection as Zara spoke first, "Your angel was definitely listening. I don't think you need to be hit with a hammer to know this was your answer."

The chatter began to heighten, and everyone felt they had to say something. Dr. Martinez then asked if there were any questions from the group.

Maya spoke up, her voice unusually hesitant. "What will you tell him? About his father?"

The room fell silent. This was the question they all had been waiting for.

Mark's face hardened slightly, but his voice stayed calm. "We'll tell him the truth when he's old enough to understand. We'll tell him that his birth mother was very young, hurt by an older boy who abused her trust. We'll tell him that none of it was her fault. And we'll tell him that from something terrible, something beautiful was born—him."

"We won't hide his origin story," Loral said. "But we also won't let it define him. He'll know he was wanted deeply. He'll know he was loved by Jalin enough to give him a different life. And he'll know he has a whole community of people who watched over his beginning—a sisterhood."

They talked for two hours. About practical matters—the birth plan, hospital procedures, the moment when Jalin would hand over her son, and Mark and Loral would become parents. About emotional issues—how Jalin would cope, how the visits would feel, and what would happen if it became too hard.

But mostly, they told stories. The Sweet Seven Plus shared memories of Jalin from before, of who she had been at eleven, twelve, and thirteen. Mark and Loral shared their dreams for who this child might become. Dr. Martinez wove it all together, creating a tapestry where past and future met in a moment that was both heartbreaking and hopeful.

As the evening came to an end, Loral reached into her bag. "We brought something. For all of you."

She took out a small velvet pouch and opened it, displaying eight delicate silver bracelets, each featuring a tiny charm—a guardian angel.

"We wanted you to have something to commemorate this," Mark explained. "To remind you that you're all connected to this little boy, that you all played a role in his story."

They accepted the bracelets silently, slipping them onto wrists that were no longer the wrists of children but not yet those of women either—caught in between, like everything else in their lives.

There's one more thing," Jalin said, her voice thick. "I want to tell you what I've decided about his name."

Mark and Loral exchanged a glance, and Angelina realized they already knew, that this had been decided together.

"If it's okay with Mark and Loral," Jalin continued, "I'd like his middle name to be Raphael. It means 'God heals.' Because maybe... maybe something good can come from something bad. Maybe he can be the healing."

"And we'd like his first name to be Jay," Mark said. "J-A-Y. Simple, strong. And it honors Jalin, carries a piece of her with him always."

"Jay Raphael Brooks," Dr. Martinez said softly. "It's beautiful."

"Jay-Ray," Keisha said suddenly, and they all turned to her. "That's what we'll call him. Jay-Ray."

Loral smiled, tears tracking down her cheeks. "Jay-Ray. He's going to be so loved."

It was May 31st, 11:47 p.m., the text chain had been active for hours, a lifeline between eight girls scattered across the city, all awake, all waiting.

Jalin: *Contractions are 5 minutes apart. Mom is taking me to the hospital. This is really happening.*

Maya: *You've got this. We're all here with you, even if we can't be THERE with you.*

Angelina: *You're the bravest person I know.*

Rosa: Give Jay-Ray a kiss from his aunts before you hand him over.

Imani: *Praying for you. For all of you.*

Zara: *I'm drawing him a picture. I'll finish it before you come home.*

Keisha: *We love you so much.*

Jade: *You're going to be amazing. As a birth mother, as a big sister, as YOU.*

Jalin: *I'm so scared. What if I can't do this? What if I change my mind when I see him?*

Dr. Martinez: *(added to the chain) Jalin, whatever you feel is valid. Whatever you decide, we support you. There is no wrong answer here. Only what's right for you and for him.*

Jalin: *They're taking me in. Next time I text, I'll be a birth mother. And it's my birthday. I'm turning 14 today.*

Maya: *Happy birthday, Jalin. What a birthday gift—giving life.*

Time feels slow for the other seven aunties, but they manage to wait until 6:42 a.m. when the chat line comes alive with a ringing phone alert.

Jalin: *He's here. 6 pounds, 3 ounces. Perfect. They let me hold him for an hour. Mark and Loral are with him now. I'm okay. I'm sad, happy, empty, and full—all at once.*

Jalin: *I just realized something. Mary, Jesus's mother, she was probably 13 when she got pregnant. 14 when she gave birth. I learned that in catechism years ago but never really thought about it until now.*

Angelina: *I was just thinking the same thing.*

Maya: *The Bible never says she was assaulted, but scholars think she was probably around that age. A child herself, carrying God's son.*

Jalin: *She kept her baby. I'm giving mine away. But maybe we're both just doing what we have to do. What's right for the child, not what's easiest for us. Look how different her life was. The older man said he would be her husband so she wouldn't be stoned to death. Wow.*

Dr. Martinez: *That's a profound connection, Jalin. Mary said yes to an impossible situation. You're saying yes too—yes to life, yes to love, yes to a different path. There's holiness in that.*

Imani: *You're both mothers who loved your sons enough to let them be part of something bigger than themselves.*

Jalin: *I never thought of it that way.*

Keisha: *How are Mark and Loral?*

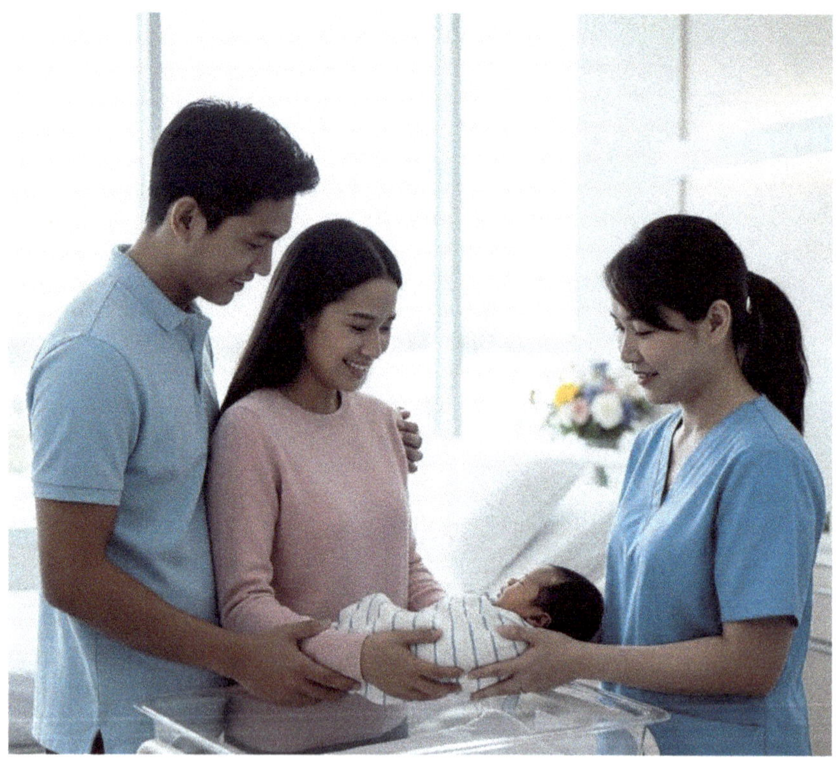

***Jalin:** Crying, smiling, completely in love. Loral keeps saying thank you as if I'm giving her a gift straight from God. Mark can't stop staring at him. They're going to be good parents. I made the right choice.*

***Zara:** When can we see him?*

***Jalin:** Mark and Loral are taking him home today. They said they'll bring him back Friday evening. They want you all to meet him properly—to see him in their arms, where he belongs.*

Friday evening didn't take long to arrive. The conference room had been decorated again, this time with balloons in soft blues and whites, and a banner that read "Welcome Jay-Ray" in Rosa's careful calligraphy. Gifts were piled in a corner—onesies, books, and stuffed animals from eight girls who were learning what it meant to be aunts in a way no fourteen-year-old should have to learn. They were now all fourteen, and look how much had happened in that year between thirteen and fourteen.

But they were all here. Together. Waiting.

When Mark and Loral arrived, carrying a car seat with one-week-old Jay Raphael Brooks, the room fell silent with a reverence usually reserved for churches.

He was tiny. Perfect. Unaware that his existence was the result of trauma, that his life had been chosen despite impossible odds, and that eight teenage girls along with two adoptive parents watched him breathe as if he were an absolute miracle.

Because he was.

Loral lifted him from the car seat, and Jalin stepped forward first. This was her right. Her moment.

"Hi, Jay-Ray," she whispered, her finger touching his tiny hand. "I'm... I'm Jalin. Your birth mom. But you can call me your big sister when you're old enough to call me anything."

His hand was wrapped around her finger with that automatic grip newborns have, and Jalin's tears fell onto his blanket.

"I love you," she told him. "I will always love you. And I gave you to the best parents in the world. You're going to be so happy."

One by one, they held him, these eight girls forming a circle around a tiny boy. They whispered promises—to remember him, to visit when they could, to be the cool aunts who spoiled him and told him stories about his brave birth mother.

Mark and Loral watched with the generous hearts of people who understood that love multiplies rather than divides, that Jay-Ray gaining eight fiercely protective honorary aunts only made him richer.

"We wanted to invite you all to our home," Loral said, once Jay-Ray was back in her arms, content and sleeping. "The last week of August, just before school starts again. We have a pool—it's nothing fancy, but it's summer, and we thought maybe you could all come swim. Bring your mothers if you'd like. We want them to know us too, to see that Jay-Ray is safe and loved."

We want you to feel comfortable, "Mark added." To see where he'll grow up. To know you're always welcome in his life.

"A pool party," Jade said, a smile breaking through. "For Jay-Ray's aunts."

Loral confirmed, "For Jay-Ray's aunts."

They made plans—exchanging addresses, arranging carpools, and coordinating the logistics of eight teenage girls and their mothers heading to a Miami suburb for a pool party with a three-month-old baby and his adoptive parents.

It should have been absurd. Maybe it was absurd.

But it was also exactly right.

As they got ready to leave, Dr. Martinez pulled them aside, her professional facade slipping to reveal something more personal.

I want you all to understand what you witnessed today," she said. "Jalin made a choice that most adults couldn't make. She chose life for her baby when she could have chosen otherwise. She chose to endure nine months of physical changes, social stigma, and emotional turmoil. And then she chose to place him with parents who could give him what she couldn't.

That's not weakness. That's not giving up. That's sacrificial love—like the love Mary showed when she said yes to the angel that appeared to her during the night, or when she stood at the foot of the cross and watched her son die for others.

She looked at Jalin specifically. "You were fourteen when you gave birth, just like Mary probably was. You've walked a path that echoes hers—young, afraid, but ultimately faithful to what you believed was right. That's sacred, Jalin. Don't let anyone tell you otherwise."

Jalin nodded, unable to speak, as the Sweet Seven Plus gathered around her—their sister, their warrior, their Madonna in cargo pants and a T-shirt that read "Nevertheless, She Persisted."

Outside, the June evening was warm and full of summer's promise. Fireflies blinked in the hedges. Somewhere, an ice cream truck played its tinny song. The world kept turning, indifferent to the small miracles happening in conference rooms and hospital delivery suites.

But eight of them knew. They had witnessed something sacred.

A fourteen-year-old girl, a newborn boy, and the people who loved them both—imperfectly, fiercely, with a devotion that went beyond biology and circumstance.

They left together, arms linked, with their guardian angel bracelets catching the light on their wrists.

Behind them, Mark and Loral buckled Jay-Ray into his car seat for the drive back to Miami, returning to the home where he would grow up surrounded by sea turtle stories, library books, and the knowledge that somewhere, a young woman loved him enough to let him go.

And somewhere in the universe, perhaps Mary understood. Maybe she looked down at another fourteen-year-old mother who'd chosen life against all odds and whispered: Well done, daughter. Well done.

END Of CHAPTER EIGHT

Educational Note: Open adoption has become more common, enabling birth mothers to keep varying levels of contact with the children they place for adoption. The details are negotiated between birth parents and adoptive parents, often with help from adoption agencies or counselors. These arrangements can include letters, photos, visits, and other types of contact.

For young women facing unplanned pregnancies, especially those resulting from sexual assault, the decision about whether to parent, place for adoption, or terminate the pregnancy is deeply personal. All choices deserve respect and support. Organizations are available to provide counseling, resources, and assistance regardless of which path a young woman chooses.

If you or someone you know is dealing with an unexpected pregnancy and needs help, contact:

- *National Sexual Assault Hotline: 1-800-656-4673*
- *Planned Parenthood: 1-800-230-7526*
- *National Adoption Center: 1-800-TO-ADOPT*
- *Local crisis pregnancy centers (assess carefully; some mainly promote anti-abortion views. In some states, anti-abortion care is mandatory, and this is not an option.)*

Every situation is unique, and every young woman deserves accurate information, compassionate support, and the freedom to choose what's best for her body and her future, where the law allows.

FINAL NOTES

When your Life Needs More Help

breaking free of the Trap

Understanding the trap is the first step. Now, let's talk about how to avoid it, escape from it, or help friends caught in it.

Prevention: Recognizing Grooming Early

The earlier you recognize grooming, the easier it is to keep yourself safe:

The Specialness Pattern:

- Does this adult make you feel uniquely special in ways that separate you from others?
- Are you being told you're "different" from other girls your age?
- Is the relationship framed as unique and unusually deep?

The Secrecy Pattern:

- Are you keeping aspects of this relationship secret?
- Has the adult asked you not to tell your parents about things?
- Do you feel like you can't tell friends about your interactions?

The Isolation Pattern:

- Are you spending less time with friends or family?
- Has the adult criticized your other relationships?
- Do you feel like you have to choose between this adult and others?

The boundary Pattern:

- Has touching occurred that made you uncomfortable?
- Have conversations turned sexual or overly personal?
- Do you feel like boundaries are being pushed gradually?

If you notice these signs, you're being groomed. Take action now before it escalates.

What To Do If you Recognize Grooming

1. **Trust your Instincts**
   If something feels wrong, it is wrong. Your gut instinct is your brain's warning signal spotting danger. Don't dismiss it.

2. **Name It**
   Say to yourself: "This is grooming. This person is behaving predatorily toward me."

   Naming it makes it real and harder to deny. If you have a support group at school, join it and see what others are doing to stay safe.

3. **Create Distance**
   - Avoid being alone with this person
   - Stop responding to private messages
   - Make excuses not to accept rides or invitations
   - Reestablish connections with friends and family

   Most organizations advise you to confide in a trusted adult, as this is the most important step. In some communities, this may be true; however, history shows it can also lead to greater danger. Recently, the victims of the Epstein rapes were not taken seriously by the

FBI. You will need to decide if you have a special support group of girls like Angelina did.

If not, contact the appropriate adult who works directly with cases of young people's abuse. The list is found in several places throughout this book. So, turn to those trusted adults for support.

4. **Document Everything**
    - Save messages, turn your phone to record.
    - Write down incidents with dates and times
    - Keep gifts or evidence
    - Document your account while details are fresh
    - Only tell your support group what you are doing.

5. **Prepare for the Predator's Response**

    When you create distance or tell someone, the predator may:

    - Try to guilt you ("I thought we were friends")
    - Try to scare you ("No one will believe you")
    - Try to blame you ("You wanted this")
    - Escalate attempts to contact you

This is predictable predator behavior. It doesn't mean you made a mistake. It means you're escaping, and they're trying to pull you back in.

If It's Already Gone further

If sexual abuse has already occurred:

you are not responsible. The predator is.

Here's what you need to know:

1. **It's not too late to tell.**
    No matter how long it's been, no matter how many times it happened, no matter what you did or didn't do, you can tell someone now.

- RAINN (1-800-656-4673)
- Childhelp National Child Abuse Hotline (1-800-422-4453)
- Crisis Text Line (text HOME to 741741)
- School counselors trained in abuse response
- Therapists who specialize in victims' trauma

2. **you should not be punished**

   You might worry about getting into trouble for keeping secrets, going along with things, or not stopping it sooner. But someone with more power and experience was manipulating you, and the right adults will understand that. Don't tell just any adult. That might make you feel worse.

3. **Telling might be hard, but silence is harder**

   Keeping the secret protects the predator and harms you. Telling is frightening, but it's the way to healing when you find the right person to share with.

4. **you deserve support**

   There are people whose job it is to help survivors of abuse:

   - RAINN (1-800-656-4673)
   - Childhelp National Child Abuse Hotline (1-800-422-4453)
   - Crisis Text Line (text HOME to 741741)
   - School counselors trained in abuse response
   - Therapists who specialize in victims' trauma

Helping a friend

If you suspect a friend is being groomed or abused, help them get this information.

1. **Don't confront the predator**

   You're not responsible for stopping them, and it could put your friend in danger. The girls in this story had a specific plan, and most of the time they had the right adults with them, like the

"Men-in-Black." If a predator is cornered or confronted with their own words, they may become violent, and you need to have an adult ready to help you, as seen in the "intervention process."

2. **Talk to your friend**
   - Express concern: "I've noticed some things that worry me."
   - Ask gentle questions: "How do you feel about your relationship with [person]?"
   - Listen without judgment: "I believe you. This isn't your fault."
   - Offer perspective: "What [person] is doing sounds like grooming."

3. **Tell the right adult**
   - RAINN (1-800-656-4673)
   - Childhelp National Child Abuse Hotline (1-800-422-4453)
   - Crisis Text Line (text HOME to 741741)
   - School counselors trained in abuse response
   - Therapists who specialize in victims' trauma

4. **4. Stay available**

Your friend might pull away initially. Keep reaching out. Let them know you care. Don't abandon them.

Special Note #1: *The idea that predators will always get what they deserve is incorrect. Young girls' reports are often ignored. In some cases, confronting the predator can harm the family in various ways, and it may be better to provide support rather than involve the legal system. We have many stories showing how the legal system can fail young girls and worsen their families' situations.*

Historically, telling a trusted adult about being groomed was seen as an immediate and clear response. However, there is no law against being groomed, and by the time the assault occurs, it can be too late. Girls who haven't had early support may lack guidance if they haven't had a team helping them through grooming. When told to share concerns with a trusted adult, many continue the abuse. If you're talking about adults, look for counselors who specialize in abuse or police units that handle victims' crimes. Avoid any so-called "trusted adult." Use the contact numbers provided here or make sure you're reaching out to qualified professionals who specialize in helping abuse victims.

- RAINN (1-800-656-4673)
- Childhelp National Child Abuse Hotline
- (1-800-422-4453)
- Crisis Text Line (text HOME to 741741)
- School counselors trained in abuse response
- Therapists who specialize in victims' trauma

Special Note #2: *One more thing about boys. This story does not suggest that all boys and men are evil or unable to control their desires. They have other options, and you do not need to be the victim of their urges or of what's going on in their heads. They may have unique struggles, but they need to find ways to manage them. That is something boys have to deal with. As girls, you also have complicated things to manage. That is what you can focus on.*

Remember: The Trap Can be broken

Thousands of girls have escaped grooming situations. Thousands have healed from abuse. Thousands have moved on to live full, healthy lives. The trap is strong, but it's not unbreakable.

You possess more power than the predator wants you to believe. You have more support than you might realize. You have the right to be safe, and you can gather the strength to break free.

Be strong—be courageous—embrace your power as a Goddess who knows she carries the Divine within her, which we call the Holy Spirit. Remember, angels surround you, so ask for their help when needed. Change the title of future books from "When Turning 13 Triggers the Devil," to "When 13 Triggers the Goddess Within."

ABOUT THE AUTHOR

Dennis Ondrejka, Ph.D., MSN, RN, D.div.(h)

Dr. Dennis Ondrejka is known as a "Liberator of Human Potential." With a broad background in academia and healthcare, experience facilitating men's and couples' weekend retreats, and experience as a HoKomI-Shadow clinician, Dr. Ondrejka is a professor of nursing, with a master's degree and many years of experience in the world of "Community Health or Public Health". This is an area that deals with every aspect of a community's risks, including trafficking, abuse, and deaths. He has spent years of study and teaching on ways to address this, but the resources have always been fragile at best. Systems are failing our young, and this book is aimed at fighting one area using knowledge—understanding grooming. It is aimed at young women first for a couple of reasons, with the primary reason being the similarities seen for the past 2000 years in how they might be targeted by cultures, religions, and perpetrators. Dr. Ondrejka does not believe the abuse of boys is structured in the same way, and is a different story to be told.

You can contact Dr. Ondrejka for webinars, workshops, and 2 to 5-day retreats at: Ctrlaltdelete1776@gmail.com or visit the member page and request your interests at www.transcendentseekers.com

Song to match the readers content

www.transcendentseekers.com

BIN TRAVERLER FORM

Cut By:______ Yeely ____ #5 ____Qty___ 60 ___Date___ 08.18.26 ___

Scanned By:______________________Qty_________Date______________

Scanned Batch ID's

__________________   __________________   __________________

Notes / Exceptions

____